Critical Guides to Spanish Texts

EDITED BY J. E. VAREY AND A. D. DE\

Critical Guides to Spanish Texts

11 Cela: La colmena

C. J. CELA

La Colmena

David Henn

**Assistant Professor of Spanish in the
University of Victoria, British Columbia**

Grant & Cutler Ltd *in association with*
Tamesis Books Ltd   1974

ISBN 0 900411 88 0

I.S.B.N. 84-399-2688-X

DEPÓSITO LEGAL: V. 3.403 - 1974

Printed in Spain by
Artes Gráficas Soler, S. A., Valencia
for
GRANT AND CUTLER LTD
11, BUCKINGHAM STREET, LONDON, W.C.2.

Contents

Explanatory Note

This book includes an expanded version of material which appeared previously in three articles published in *Neophilologus*, LV (1971), 142-149; *Forum for Modern Language Studies*, VIII (1972), 304-319; and *Romance Notes*, XIII (1971-72), 414-418. I am indebted to the Editors of the three journals for giving me permission to include this material in the present volume.

All page references to the text of the novel are from the twelfth edition, contained in the *Obra completa*, tomo VII, *Tres novelas más* (Barcelona: Destino, 1969). Other single page references, to the *Notas* to the various editions of *La colmena* or to other introductory essays, are also from Volume VII of the *Obra completa*.

The figures in parentheses in italic type refer to the numbered items in the Bibliographical Note; the italic figure is followed by a page reference.

I Introduction

Camilo José Cela was born in Iria-Flavia, Galicia, in 1916 and achieved fame and some notoriety with the publication of his first novel, *La familia de Pascual Duarte*, in 1942. Since then, his literary production has been prolific, ranging from novels, short stories and travel books, to poetry, critical studies and, more recently, the early volumes of the *Diccionario secreto*. In 1956 Cela founded the literary review *Papeles de Son Armadans* and has remained its editor since that date. Formal recognition of his contribution to Spanish letters came in 1957 when he was elected to the Real Academia Española and thus became, at the age of forty-one, the youngest member of that august group. Cela's career has been marked by frequent controversy over the quality or content of his work, or over his forthright views on his own talent and that of others, and his pronouncements on literature in general. There can be little doubt that he is the most widely known of the Spanish writers who began their careers after the Civil War and equally little doubt that he is also the best. With a characteristic candour and arrogance that has infuriated so many on countless occasions, Cela has even remarked:

> Me considero el más importante novelista español desde el 98, y me espanta el considerar lo fácil que me resultó. Pido perdón por no haberlo podido evitar.[1]

Although his "me espanta el considerar lo fácil que me resultó" is obviously ambiguous, it is indeed a sad reality that post-Civil War Spain can claim few novels or novelists of consequence.

To those who awaited with eager curiosity a Spanish literature inspired by the conflict of 1936-1939, the publication of *La familia de Pascual Duarte* came as something of an unexpected and bewildering shock. Here was a powerful and well written novel which was an account not of glory or sacrifice in the bitter conflict that had rent the country and aroused passions throughout the world, but rather the memoirs of the squalid life of an Extremaduran peasant, written

---

[1] C. J. Cela, *Baraja de invenciones* (Valencia: Editorial Castalia, 1953), p. 8.

from the condemned cell. The tone of the novel is brutal; Cela had asked Pío Baroja to write a prologue to *Pascual Duarte* and the latter responded: "–No, mire, si usted quiere que lo lleven a la cárcel, vaya" (*16*, 84). Baroja may have been excessively cautious; however, in 1943 copies of the novel were confiscated although the action was largely futile since so few copies of the first two editions remained unsold. *Pascual Duarte* brought Cela to prominence and also gave rise to a new -*ismo* in the literary vocabulary, *tremendismo*. The term is intended to signify the depiction of brutality (both physical and mental) and the savouring of that brutality. In a prefatory essay to *Mrs. Caldwell habla con su hijo* (1953), entitled "Algunas palabras al que leyere", Cela roundly rejects both the term and the vogue:

> Los novelistas de receta, al ver que [*Pascual Duarte*] había tenido cierto buen éxito . . . empezaron a seguir sus huellas y nació el tremendismo, que, entre otras cosas, es una estupidez de tomo y lomo, una estupidez sólo comparable a la estupidez del nombre que se le da (973).

Cela's next two novels, *Pabellón de reposo* (1943) and *Nuevas andanzas y desventuras de Lazarillo de Tormes* (1944), are both far removed from the theme, style and tone of *Pascual Duarte*. They deal with, respectively, life and death in a sanatorium (Cela had previously entered a sanatorium twice for treatment of tuberculosis) and the adventures of a modern Lazarillo de Tormes. Neither novel had the impact of *Pascual Duarte* but both indicated that Cela was obviously developing as a novelist and that he was not going to become a "novelista de receta". His most notable achievement of the late 1940s was *Viaje a la Alcarria* (1948), a vivid, sensitive and beautifully written account of a tour made by the author through the Alcarria region. This travel book not only recalled the best of this *genre* as practised by Azorín, Unamuno or Ciro Bayo but also revealed an additional facet of Cela's literary talent. In the meantime, Cela had been working since 1945 on *La colmena* and by 1950 felt that it was finally ready for publication.

La colmena was first published in Buenos Aires in 1951, after Cela had spent more than four years trying to have various drafts of the novel accepted by the Spanish censor. In his essay "Historia incompleta de unas páginas zarandeadas" Cela summarizes the history of the manuscript and his struggle to get it into print: "En el 1946, empezó mi lucha con la censura, guerra en la que perdí todas las

batallas menos la última" (39). Although the author does not specify
the reasons for the censor's disapproval, it is likely that the problem
arose from the tone of the novel as much as from its content. In
1950 Cela made a final attempt to have the novel published in Spain
and, when this failed, gave the manuscript to Emecé of Buenos
Aires. The Argentinian censor, however, withheld his *imprimatur*
until certain modifications were agreed to and, finally, in 1951 "el
libro pudo publicarse en una versión bastante correcta" (45-6). Some
years later publication of *La colmena* in Spain was permitted and
the twelfth edition (contained in the *Obra completa*, tomo VII,
1969) includes and indicates material omitted from previous editions.
Such material reveals both the extent to which the Spanish censor
has become less stringent and also the degree of tolerance accorded
to Cela and which is often denied to his less well known colleagues.
Much of the language of Cela's latest major work, *San Camilo, 1936*,
published in 1969, also testifies to the fact that he is now able to take
advantage of his position as the recognized *doyen* of post-Civil War
Spanish writers by extracting the maximum freedom that the censor
will allow.

Eugenio de Nora describes *La colmena* as "la novela más valiosa
y significativa publicada en España después de 1936" (*8*, 75) and
Gerald Brown comments on the influence that the novel was to have
on Cela's younger colleagues:

> The lead that Cela gave them was in taking as his theme the
> bitter reality of life in post-war Spain, a hungry, suffering, cynical,
> brutalized world. After *La colmena* there occurred a sudden
> flowering (in spite of the censor's energetic prunings) of young
> literary talent dedicated to the cause of exposing, or at least
> testifying to, the miseries of Spanish life, and expressing itself in
> the stark, objectively realistic manner which the subject seemed
> to demand (*7*, 147).

With regard to those authors whose work may have influenced Cela's
own writing in general or *La colmena* in particular, various names
have been tossed (usually casually) into the hat, including those of
Galdós, Valle-Inclán, Pío Baroja, John Dos Passos and Aldous Huxley.
Major links have yet to be demonstrated. Considering the sheer
quantity and variety of Cela's work and the depth and breadth of his
acquaintance with Spanish literature, it would indeed be surprising
if his writing showed no traces or hints of the influence of other

writers. However, Cela has normally been more interested in experi-
mentation than imitation. D. W. Foster says of the structure of his
novels:

> Cela's novels are a critic's delight in that the author has followed
> so many different procedures that have resulted, in turn, in so
> many different forms. If nothing else, Cela has become Spain's
> most restless and versatile novelistic technician (*9*, 15).

Olga Prjevalinsky makes a similar point:

> La tarea de escribir —aventura intelectual para Cela— es
> incitación que le lleva a proyectar en diversos géneros de novela
> su arte riguroso y versátil, geométrico y huidizo. Con espíritu
> genuinamente deportivo emprende la creación de obras de estilo
> diferente.[2]

Brown's comment that "Cela has been one of the very few truly
experimental novelists in post-war Spain" (*7*, 145) is a statement
that should be borne in mind when considering Cela's work. His
experiments have not always achieved success. Much has been
expected of him and when Cela has written works that do not attain
the stature of *La familia de Pascual Duarte* or *La colmena* most
critics have expressed a disappointed concern whilst some have
obviously chuckled their way to the typewriter.

Since 1951 Cela has written prolifically, including novels, short
stories and travel books, but has, sadly, devoted too little of his time
to the novel. His much heralded *San Camilo, 1936* (1969) sold well
but generally received a lukewarm reception from the reviewers, who
usually compared it (and unfavourably) with *La colmena. La colmena*
is still widely regarded as Cela's masterpiece and often the masterpiece of post-Civil War prose fiction. Cela has written much about
his own work and before embarking on this study of *La colmena*, I
feel that it is both fitting and necessary to let the author introduce
his novel. In "Algunas palabras al que leyere", he writes:

> En *La colmena* no presto atención sino a tres días de la vida
> de la ciudad, o de un estrato determinado de la ciudad, que es un
> poco la suma de todas las vidas que bullen en sus páginas, unas
> vidas grises, vulgares y cotidianas, sin demasiada grandeza, esa es
> la verdad. *La colmena* es una novela sin héroe, en la que todos sus
> personajes, como el caracol, viven inmersos en su propia insig-
> nificancia (976-7).

2El sistema estético de Camilo José Cela (Valencia: Editorial Castalia, 1966),
p. 16.

II Background: the aftermath of war

In the introductory comments (later termed *Nota a la primera edición*) to the first edition of *La colmena*, Cela indicates a fairly precise historical setting for his novel: "Su acción discurre en Madrid —en 1942— y entre un torrente, o una colmena, de gentes que a veces son felices, y a veces, no" (958). Cela's fifth novel, *Mrs. Caldwell habla con su hijo*, appeared in 1953 and included a prefatory essay entitled "Algunas palabras al que leyere" in which Cela expounds some of his ideas on the novel in general and also discusses his own work. With reference to *La colmena*, he states: "*La colmena* es la novela de la ciudad, de una ciudad concreta y determinada, Madrid, en una época cierta y no imprecisa, 1942, y con casi todos sus personajes, sus muchos personajes, con nombres y dos apellidos, para que no haya dudas" (975). However, in the "Prólogo a la edición rumana de *La colmena*", first written in 1965 and included in the *Obra completa*, tomo VII, we read: ". . . de lo que aquí se trata es más bien del producto de una lengua y una historia todavía muy cercanas a nosotros: el español popular y la ciudad de Madrid en torno a los años 1940 ó 42, hace ahora ya un cuarto de siglo" (967). From this it would appear that a precise time setting for *La colmena* is, perhaps, relatively unimportant. Unfortunately though, one cannot even be guided by Cela's latest indication and settle for the 1940-1942 period. The reason for this is found in the text of the novel. Although the Second World War was being fought at the time in question, there are few references to it, save the occasional allusion to the fortunes of the Axis powers. In Chapters I to VI there are, in fact, only four references to the conflict and none of these is to specific events. The *Final* contains the sole mention of historical events either connected with or part of the World War. In a brief scene, Rómulo, a secondhand bookseller, glances at his newspaper:

Rómulo, en su librería de lance, lee el periódico.
Londres.   Radio Moscú anuncia que la conferencia entre Churchill, Roosevelt y Stalin se ha celebrado en Teherán hace unos días.
— ¡Este Churchill es el mismo diablo!   ¡Con la mano de años que tiene y largándose de un lado para otro como si fuese un

pollo!
   Cuartel General del Führer. En la región de Gomel, del sector central del frente del este, nuestras fuerzas han evacuado los puntos de . . .
   — ¡Huy, huy!   ¡A mí esto me da muy mala espina!
   Londres. El presidente Roosevelt llegó a la isla de Malta a bordo de su avión gigante Douglas.
   ¡Qué tío!   ¡Pondría una mano en el fuego porque ese aero-planito tiene hasta retrete! (*Final*, 353).

All three events mentioned in this passage took place toward the end of 1943. The first plenary session of the Teheran Conference was held on 28th November and the conference ended on 1st December with a joint statement signed by Roosevelt, Stalin and Churchill. The Russian town of Gomel, which had been in German hands for more than two years, was recaptured by the Red Army on 26th November and, finally, President Roosevelt paid a three-hour visit to Malta on 8th December. Thus, these events reported in *La colmena* indicate that Cela has inadvertently set his novel in late 1943. However, the exact date of the action is not, I think, of primary importance and the reader should rather view the people portrayed in *La colmena* as a group facing the problems and illustrating the condition of a section of Madrid society during the years immediately following the end of the Spanish Civil War.

   On 1st April 1939 Generalissimo Francisco Franco announced the victory of his Nationalist forces in the Civil War that had racked Spain for nearly three years —a war which had aroused the passions of many beyond the borders of Spain as well as causing the direct intervention of Germany, Italy and Soviet Russia. In addition, thousands of Europeans and North Americans went to Spain, the majority to fight for the Republic, and many of these joined the famed International Brigades. The cost of the war had been great. Estimates of the number who perished in the conflict, both military and civilian, have ranged as high as one million. Hugh Thomas has suggested that a realistic figure for deaths directly and indirectly attributable to the war would be 500,000. Thomas also mentions the many disabled and the 340,000 persons exiled at the end of the war (5, 758-9). These figures serve to give a rough idea of the human suffering that the Spanish Civil War caused. Other legacies included ravaged industries, communications and personal property, and an exhausted economy.

Franco's first task was to consolidate his victory by exercising to the full the military and political power at his disposal, in order to ensure that his position could be challenged neither from within his victorious National Movement nor by the vanquished Republicans. He was also faced with the task of rebuilding the economy. Soon, with the outbreak of the Second World War in September 1939, he found himself engaged in critical (and skilful) diplomatic manoeuvring in order to resist the pressure of Adolf Hitler, aimed at forcing Spain to declare war on France and England. Franco was wise enough to realize that Spain was in no position to engage in yet another war and he also knew that he must consolidate his own position within Spain and thus ensure that the insurrection of July 1936 (of which he was a principal architect) would yield long-term benefits for both himself and the country.

In February 1939, with the Nationalist victory imminent, Franco issued the *Ley de Responsabilidad Política*. Brian Crozier's summary of this law and his description of the machinery that was later set up to enforce it indicate the ominous threat posed to many Spaniards by a law "punishing subversion between 1 October 1934 (the time of the Asturian revolution) and 18 July 1936 (the day of the Nationalist rising); and punishing opposition to the National Movement thereafter. On 14 March of the same year, a special Tribunal of Political Responsibilities was set up to administer the new Law. Simultaneously, military tribunals were set up in towns and cities that had emerged from Republican rule, to which all witnesses of Republican crimes were summoned to give evidence" (*1*, 295-6). Thomas states that "Nearly all officers of the Republican Army were shot if captured . . . On the other hand, the rank and file were generally released" (*5*, 760). This was, of course, provided that there were no crimes proven against these members of the rank and file. Otherwise, Thomas writes, "the victors showed no charity" (*5*, 761). In this connection, George Hills states: "The victors went on between 1939 and 1943 to execute over 40,000 of the defeated and to sentence a quarter of a million to varying terms of imprisonment" (*3*, 230). Precise figures are understandably impossible to obtain and Crozier, whilst admitting the difficulty of finding reliable figures, feels that over this four-year period as many as 200,000 may have died in Nationalist prisons through execution or disease (*1*, 296). What is

certain is that the years following the end of the war were marked
by a considerable amount of retribution which must have resulted
in many innocent Spaniards suffering at the hands of the new regime
and must also have caused a good deal of apprehension to both
innocent and "guilty" alike. Although a *denuncia* might well bring
a criminal or opponent of the National Movement to the attention of
the authorities it could also be used as a drastic and deadly means of
attempting to settle scores of a personal nature.

Another grave problem facing the new regime was the economic
exhaustion produced by the Civil War and aggravated after April
1939 by factors beyond the control of Franco and his government.
Stanley Payne comments: "By the autumn of 1940, the Spanish
economy was in desperate straits. The disruption of international
commerce brought about by the [Second World] war severely
hampered reconstruction in Spain, which faced great obstacles in any
event. Weather conditions deteriorated in the early 1940's, by
which time economic deprivation was actually worse than it had
been during the Civil War" (*4*, 29). Controls and rationing were
introduced but these were generally ineffective, and "by the early
1940's, a massive black market, mainly in foodstuffs, had developed"
(*4*, 55). In November 1941, after yet another bad harvest, it was
announced that black marketeers could be punished by death. However, the law of supply and demand ensured the continuation of a
flourishing black market and the words *estraperlo* and *estraperlista*
were very much part of the post-war vocabulary.[3] By 1943 the
situation was beginning to improve; the harvest of 1942 was better
than those of the immediate post-war years and also the British
Government, at last realizing the gravity of Spain's economic position,
became less stringent with regard to the issuing of Navicerts.[4] Also, in

---

[3]"Estraperlo" is derived from "straperlo" – the name of a particular type of
roulette wheel which the Dutch financier Daniel Strauss, with the complicity
of several Radical ministers, tried to introduce into Spain in 1934. A scandal
concerning this erupted in 1935 and caused the resignation of several of the
politicians implicated. Subsequently, "estraperlo" signified a financial scandal
involving members of the government and later became the word for "black
market".

[4]The abbreviated version of "Navigation Certificates". These were used by the
Royal Navy in both World Wars and were issued to neutral vessels when the
Navy was satisfied that such vessels were not carrying cargoes which were
directly or indirectly related to the war effort.

1943 Spain began to export wolfram (used in the manufacture of aircraft engines) and thereby earned some valuable foreign currency. However, the economic situation was still precarious, and "another nine years were to pass before food supplies returned to pre-1936 levels" (*3*, 246).

In addition, economic hardship, political repression and the ordeal of nearly three years of civil war took their toll in terms of the mental state and moral outlook of many of the Spanish people. Thomas Hamilton, who was, between August 1939 and July 1941, correspondent in Spain for the *New York Times*, writes of "the general lowering of moral standards which followed the end of the civil war. It was every man for himself, with no mercy for the poor, the weak, or the scrupulous" (*2*, 170). He also describes "the general corruption which resulted from the successful effort of the wealthy and strong not to accept the hardships produced by a war that was intended merely to restore their position under the monarchy" (*2*, 171). Finally, Hamilton stresses the obvious importance of money in this society, mentioning that by 1941 the cost of food (including the black market rates) was three or four times what it had been in 1936, and shortages were frequent in almost all other commodities: "Money was able to accomplish almost anything in Franco Spain. This was true despite the fact that there was not enough of anything that people wanted, from food, apartments, clothing, public utilities, to the least important details of existence" (*2*, 171). Thus, for many, the immediate post-war years marked a period of struggle, hardship, uncertainty, apprehension and fear. For those more fortunate, it was a time when money or position could make life tolerable or even pleasant and also a time when these people would often ostentatiously indulge in the benefits within their reach, and thus emphasize the contrast between their condition and that of their less fortunate fellows. However, it would be an over-simplification to assume that the middle classes prospered whilst the working classes suffered. Good fortune, determination and scruples (or the lack of them) were also important factors in the struggle for survival or a comfortable life. Stanley Payne describes the situation as follows: "The 1940's were not merely a time of social problems and depressed living standards for the working classes alone. General economic prostration and rapid price increases also made life increasingly difficult for the

middle classes, most of whom had supported the Nationalists during
the Civil War. Throughout that decade, many important articles
could only be acquired in adequate quantity on the country's
flourishing black market. In coping with this situation, a certain
amount of change took place in the composition of the lower middle
classes. Persons who had supported the Republic or could not deal
with the new economic pressures sometimes went under, to be
replaced by those who had made good on the black market. A
smaller number of skilled workers, especially among those who had
the 'good fortune' to be pressed into service on the winning side in
the war, managed to elevate themselves into the middle classes"
(*4*, 75-6).

La colmena is not a novel about the Spanish Civil War. It contains
relatively few specific references to the conflict and, surprisingly,
none to the siege of Madrid, the defence of which Raymond Carr has
termed "the central epic of the war".[5] It is rather a novel which
displays the attitudes and actions of a section of post-war Madrid
society which is faced with physical hardship and the monotony of
a grey and often empty existence. The people seen are frequently
amoral, suspicious and selfish. There are occasional glimpses of
moral fibre and occasional signs of altruism, and notes of optimism.
In general, however, the impression created is that of a society,
often physically, and usually spiritually, exhausted. Whether Cela
has intended the reader to assume that the society he portrays is
simply the product of a war and its aftermath or whether the
attitudes displayed are meant to indicate a more profound and more
lasting social problem is largely a matter for personal interpretation.
I believe that the latter is probably the case. The overall tone of
La colmena is pessimistic and this pessimism is conveyed largely by
the impression that the majority of the characters encountered in
the novel show little sign that they desire to face the challenge that
adversity has posed for them and prefer, instead, either to wallow in
their own apathy and stagnation or, worse, exploit their fellows as
best they can.

[5]*Spain 1808-1939* (Oxford: Clarendon Press, 1970), p. 687.

The main difficulty that confronts the reader of *La colmena* is that of relating the sequence of events as they appear in the novel to the large number of characters that participate in these events. The novel is in certain respects something of a literary jigsaw puzzle. Unfortunately, once a composite picture has emerged and the reader has managed to absorb the pattern and thematic content of the work it appears that Cela has withheld the final piece, for so we may term the unexplained and tantalizing nature of the *Final*. The significance of the *Final* will be discussed subsequently; for the moment it is sufficient to say that this brief section which ends the novel is intriguing but not, I believe, essential to an overall appreciation of *La colmena*. There is a temptation to be unduly distracted by the content of the *Final* and to seek in it either the key to the other six chapters which constitute the body of the novel, or the prelude to the next novel (which never, in any case, appeared) in the *Caminos inciertos* series, or both. It is as well to bear in mind the opening words of *La colmena*, "No perdamos la perspectiva" (49), and proceed to an examination of the novel as a whole, studying the structure or framework upon which the themes have been woven and through which the multitude of characters move.

Cela spent five years working on *La colmena* and in his *Nota a la primera edición* comments: "Su arquitectura es compleja, a mí me costó mucho trabajo hacerla" (957-8). Two years later he states: "*La colmena* es una novela reloj, una novela hecha de múltiples ruedas y piececitas que se precisan las unas a las otras para que aquello marche" (976). An examination of the complex structure of *La colmena* must begin with a scrutiny of the external structure of the novel, that is the chapter divisions within the work.

External Structure

The action of *La colmena* takes place over a period of five or six days. The novel consists of six chapters and a *Final*. The six chapters span a period of approximately two days whilst the *Final* is set three or four days later. However, the chapters are not in

chronological sequence and this poses the first structural difficulty.
The sequence presented by the individual chapters is as follows:

Chapter I	Mid-evening of day A
Chapter II	Mid to late evening of day A
Chapter III	Afternoon to early evening of day B
Chapter IV	Night of day A
Chapter V	Late afternoon to evening of day B
	(with a brief incursion into day C)
Chapter VI	Morning of day B
Final	Morning —three or four days later.

Thus to read the novel in general chronological sequence it would be
necessary to take the chapters as follows:

$$\text{I} \quad \text{II} \quad \text{IV} \quad \text{VI} \quad \text{III} \quad \text{V} \quad \textit{Final}$$

I have used the word general since although Chapters I, II and IV
cover five or six hours from mid-evening to midnight, or just after, of
the first day, they are not in strict chronological sequence. There is
a certain overlapping between Chapters I and II evidenced by Martín
Marco's ejection from doña Rosa's café midway through the first
chapter (73) and his subsequent reappearance outside the café at
the beginning of the second chapter (107). An overlap also occurs
between Chapters II and IV with Roberto González's arrival home
first mentioned in II (131) and eventually seen in IV (219). The
time, according to Filo González's comment to her brother Martín
Marco (II, 126), is around 10.30 p.m.

This overlapping also occurs *within* Chapter II. Here, Marco's
progress is followed from his ejection from the café (some time
before 9.30 which marks the close of Chapter I) until approximately
11 o'clock. He does not figure in the last third of the chapter which
centres on the discovery of the murder of the old lady, doña Margot.
This section begins with a look at Leoncio Maestre and then the
arrival home of Julián Suárez, the homosexual son of the dead
woman (II, 142). Suárez had last been seen leaving doña Rosa's
café for a waiting taxi (I, 70). Once again this must have been
before 9.30 and assuming that this was the same cab ride (and not a
particularly lengthy one), then the events described in the last part
of Chapter II would commence at some time around 9.30. This
chronological overlap within Chapter II and the times involved tend
to refute one critic's suggestion of "a strong link" between Martín

Marco and the murder of doña Margot (9, 64). Thus, Chapters I, II and IV are interlocking rather than strictly sequential, with the author discreetly indicating where the chapters are coupled.

A similar technique is used to link parts of Chapter III with Chapter V. Chapter III takes the reader to the afternoon and early evening of the second day whilst the action of V takes place during the evening of that day. However, a telephone call made by Dr Francisco Robles "a eso de las siete" (V, 292-3) is the same call received by doña Celia in Chapter III (193). Chapter V is, in any case, the most complex section of *La colmena*, with a great deal of back and forth chronological movement. The episode which dominates the fifth chapter centres on the use by don Roque Moisés and his mistress Lola, and by his daughter Julita and her *novio* Ventura Aguado, of doña Celia's *casa de citas*. Each couple is unaware of the other's use of the location. The meeting between Julita and her father on the stairs of the *casa de citas* is first mentioned as a street meeting (V, 274) and is eventually witnessed by the reader later in the chapter (V, 312). This meeting takes place during the early evening of day B. However, after the first mention of the meeting between Roque Moisés and Julita and before the actual observation of the incident, the narrative moves briefly into day C with the section commencing "Al día siguiente" (V, 282), which describes the arrival of the photograph of don Obdulio at Moisés's house. This section continues with a meeting between Julita and Ventura, where the former states: "Ayer me encontré a mi padre en la escalera" (V, 284), and concludes with Ventura sending to don Roque the photograph which Lola had originally sent to Julita (V, 285-6). The subsequent sections of the chapter then carry the reader back to the early evening of day B with a fairly precise reference to the hour of the day: "A las cinco y cuarto o cinco y media, don Francisco llega a su casa, a pasar la consulta" (V, 288).

The chapters themselves, then, do not necessarily contain a strictly chronological narrative sequence and were it not for the overlapping that occurs the reader might assume that Cela has merely chopped up and reordered the narrative movement of the novel. The reason for this deliberate reordering will be discussed subsequently when it will be shown that the thematic content of *La colmena* is consonant with and in certain respects dependent on the structure.

Thus far the external structure of *La colmena* has been discussed —that is, the sequence and relationship of the principal narrative units, the chapters. These, including the *Final*, are the seven main components of the work, components which, in general, are carefully interlocked rather than being placed adjacent to each other.

If each of these chapters is examined it will be seen that the chapter itself is composed of a series of short narrative units or fragments, each dealing with a particular moment or occasion, person or group and location, and often a detailed location, such as individual tables in doña Rosa's café in Chapter I. This chapter is, for example, composed of some forty such units, usually complete in themselves but at the same time often a development of a conversation or the product of an incident and possibly its aftermath. Here the narrative moves from table to table recording snippets of conversation in the manner of an eavesdropper, alters focus to give an overall view of the café and clients and employees, and then perhaps continues a conversation at the point at which it had been left. Thus the narration functions both spatially, continually altering the distance as well as the perspective between the reader and the action, and temporally, moving back and forth in time, giving the appearance of simultaneity of action. These narrative fragments therefore tend to reorder the chronological sequence of minutes whereas the chapters had reordered that of hours and days.

La colmena, then, may be regarded as being composed of a hierarchy of temporal units. First, the whole work encompasses a period of five or six days. Each chapter is confined to a more or less specific period of a certain day, e.g., morning or evening, and, finally, the chapters are subdivided into short moments or incidents. It is this structural flexibility that facilitates Cela's dismembering and reordering of a linear temporal movement in his novel and enables him to emphasize certain thematic aspects that emerge from his portrayal of this section of 1943 Madrid society.

Internal Structure

A carefully constructed framework lies beneath the surface of *La colmena*, a surface which at first sight appears to be little more than, as Cela himself has put it in the *Nota a la primera edición*, ". . . un torrente, o una colmena, de gentes que a veces son felices, y a veces, no" (958). There are nearly three hundred of these people in the novel although only forty or fifty of them are dealt with at any length and it is through the actions and interaction of these characters that the reader must look for the dramatic structure, the plot or narrative development of *La colmena*. It is necessary to consult once more the *Nota a la primera edición* to grasp the author's own view of his novel and to discover whether he has intended to create a work in the "traditional" vein, with a developing plot, dramatic movement and character development. Here Cela's comments suggest that he has sought to produce a work that is perhaps more a documentary in presentation and content than a piece of "traditional" prose fiction: "Mi novela *La colmena*, primer libro de la serie *Caminos inciertos*, no es otra cosa que un pálido reflejo, que una humilde sombra de la cotidiana, áspera, entrañable y dolorosa realidad ... Esta novela mía no aspira a ser más —ni menos, ciertamente— que un trozo de vida narrado paso a paso, sin reticencias, sin extrañas tragedias, sin caridad, como la vida discurre, exactamente como la vida discurre" (957). However, Cela's presentation of the many characters that figure in his novel is not as haphazard as his comments might suggest, whilst the individual existences that he records certainly do constitute a rather drab and even frightening portrayal of human experience.

The opening chapter of *La colmena* is set in doña Rosa's café and shows a section (predominantly lower middle-class) of post-Civil War Madrid society. Some thirty characters are encountered, clients and employees, and the scene is dominated by the formidable doña Rosa. She is seen conversing with some of the clients, such as the ageing prostitute Elvira, cajoling her staff and generally enjoying the power that she exercises, her prestige, and the dread that she inspires in her employees. From the outset the author evokes an atmosphere of lethargy and stagnation, an atmosphere that is sustained throughout the chapter, although with a gradually decreasing emphasis. This suggested collective malaise is examined on an individual basis, with the author not only recording many of the conversations but also informing the reader of the attitudes of, for example, Jaime Arce (I, 53), one of the regular clients, or Seoane, the café violinist (I, 105). The thunder of doña Rosa's voice and her scathing comments provide most of the brief intervals of diversion in the normally monotonous atmosphere of the café. From a technical point of view, her mobility and forthrightness stand in marked contrast to the generally static clients and their insipid conversations. This contrast is emphasized by the author moving back and forth from doña Rosa to the clients and her employees and thus coupling a change of perspective with a change of tone. The clients rarely comment on her behaviour —a notable exception being Mauricio Segovia (I, 67-8), who is not an *habitual* and therefore finds doña Rosa's tantrums, to which the regular customers and staff are accustomed, somewhat surprising. The main diversions for most of the clients are the novelties provided by Martín Marco's ejection for failure to pay or the young poet who faints. These incidents are witnessed and commented upon, and then the languid conversations are resumed as the clients look wearily about them or at one another.

Chapter I serves to stress the monotony and aimlessness of the lives of most of the café clientele (this thematic aspect of the chapter will be discussed later) and to introduce certain characters who will reappear in the novel and continue to illustrate particular themes as the reader is shown the problems confronting and weighing on many of these people. Doña Rosa's café is seldom revisited but serves as the point of departure for the narrative. Approximately one third of the characters encountered in Chapter I will not reappear in the novel (e.g. Leonardo Meléndez, Jaime Arce, Isabel Montes). Another third or so are seen perhaps two or three more times in the other chapters (e.g. don Pablo, Macario, doña Matilde) and the rest either appear infrequently but in important situations (e.g. Mario de la Vega, Consorcio López), or with more regularity but without the pre-eminence enjoyed in Chapter I (e.g. doña Rosa, Elvira). There remains Martín Marco, not named when first encountered: "Uno de los hombres que, de codos sobre el velador, ya sabéis, se sujeta la pálida frente con la mano —triste y amarga la mirada, preocupada y como sobrecogida la expresión—, habla con el camarero" (I, 71). He seems to have little more significance in Chapter I than the diversionary incident provided when he is expelled from the café. Marco is, however, central to the first two-thirds of Chapter II, reappears several times in Chapters III and V, is again pre-eminent in Chapters IV and VI, and dominates the short *Final.*

Marco is thus casually introduced to the reader midway through the first chapter; some biographical information about him is given by the author, but no more than that accorded to several other people present in the café, and he is quietly removed by the waiter, still unidentified (I, 73). The scene on the pavement outside the café between Marco and Pepe opens the second chapter with the author referring to Marco four times by name before adding at the end of this opening section of the chapter: "Martín Marco, el hombre que no ha pagado el café y que mira la ciudad como un niño enfermo y acosado, mete las manos en los bolsillos del pantalón' (II, 108).

From a structural point of view, when Marco is followed away from the café at the beginning of Chapter II the scope of the novel is about to be drastically enlarged, with the introduction of new locations and new sets of characters. The tone is also modified. There begins a certain mobility (in marked contrast to the psychologically and physically static quality of Chapter I) which will bring with it an exploration at first hand of that section of Madrid society portrayed in *La colmena*. Marco is used to initiate this outward movement in the novel; he is the technical device used by Cela to conduct the narrative away from the confines of doña Rosa's café and into the streets, homes, bars, other cafés and *casas de citas* of the city. He does not, however, become the hub of the narrative, rather a point of contact, often tenuous, between many of the locations and characters yet to be encountered.

Those characters seen in the first two-thirds of Chapter II are mostly, directly or indirectly, connected with Martín Marco. The narrative follows Marco's progress across the city from the café to the flat of his sister Filo, but always shifting from Marco to, for example, his brother-in-law Roberto González at work, or Pablo Alonso (who provides Marco with clothing and shelter) with his latest girl-friend Laurita, or Celestino Ortiz's bar, one of Martín's regular haunts. The new group encountered serves to give a different perspective to the narration, with its own distinctive problems and attitudes. Marco is the dominant figure of most of the second chapter and his recurring presence might suggest the gradual unfurling of a plot centred on him. However, Marco is rather the means by which the themes of hardship and inequality are introduced and elaborated. Chapter I had, by and large, shown doña Rosa's everyday

acquaintances, "her" people. Chapters II, IV and VI will show
Marco and many of "his" people. Themes are not illustrated by
means of a developing plot but rather through the presentation of
situations and incidents. Experiences, both minor and major, are
witnessed in what appears to be, at first sight, a fairly haphazard
manner. Marco, more often seen by the reader and more closely
scrutinized by the author than any of the other characters in *La
colmena*, frequently provides a link between many of the characters,
places and incidents in the novel. He is, however, more than a
structural device; Marco is the nearest thing to a protagonist in the
novel and it is through his experiences and acquaintances that the
author illustrates certain themes, employing series of incidents instead
of the more traditional developing plot.

Of the three people who are seen to leave the café in Chapter I,
Marco is seen again at the beginning of the second chapter whilst the
other two, Leoncio Maestre and the homosexual Julián Suárez,
reappear in the last third of the chapter which deals primarily with
the murder of doña Margot, and both are subsequently detained in
connection with this incident. The episode of the murder presents
the reactions of the dead woman's neighbours and is largely situated
in the building where the crime takes place. The murder itself is not
witnessed. The author shifts his account back and forth from the
scene of the crime to other parts of the city, but always using the
building as the base of the narrative. By means of this technique,
Cela allows the reader to keep Suárez and his boy-friend under
surveillance, shows Mauricio Segovia and his brother commenting on
these two homosexuals (II, 158), and also presents the printer
Mario de la Vega and his future employee Eloy at supper and then,
later, coming across the crowd outside the building where the murder
has taken place (II, 157). In this way the murder episode is kept in
perspective as one event in the life of a city. Also, with Leoncio
Maestre who discovers the body as he is about to return to doña
Rosa's café, and the reappearance of other characters mentioned
above, the café has been linked with the murder of the old lady. The
author has carefully prepared this link for the reader whilst showing
the characters concerned as oblivious of such a link. Therefore, up
to the end of the second chapter, Cela has presented three groups of
people (the clients of the café, Marco's acquaintances and doña

Margot's neighbours) located in different parts of the city and yet in various ways connected. Also, at this point, one-third of the way through the novel, the reader should by now be aware that no conventional plot is emerging and that given the form and content of the first two chapters the author's technique is primarily descriptive rather than concerned with dramatic elaboration.

Chapter III, chronologically subsequent to Chapters IV and VI, conducts the reader to the afternoon of the second day. The early part of the chapter consists of a series of views of leisure-time activities of some characters already encountered and some now met for the first time. In the first seven sections (III, 161-74) the narrative moves from the "café de la calle de San Bernardo" to the "lechería de la calle de Fuencarral", to a "bar de lujo . . . detrás de la Gran Vía", to doña Rosa's café, from there to Celestino Ortiz's bar and, finally, back to San Bernardo, Some familiar faces are now seen in locations different from those of their first appearance with, for example, Martín Marco in the café on San Bernardo and Pablo Alonso and Laurita in a *bar de lujo*. In this early part of the chapter, don Roque Moisés and Ventura Aguado appear for the first time. They are unacquainted with each other and remain so throughout the novel. Aguado is introduced as a friend of Marco (III, 173) and subsequently Roque's daughter Julita is identified as the *novia* of Aguado (III, 189). Thus the trio which will dominate the fifth chapter (Roque, Ventura and Julita) is introduced quite casually to the reader.

With several notable exceptions, Marco amongst them, the characters of Chapter III are predominantly bourgeois and, apart from the long section dealing with the gathering of doña Margot's neighbours (III, 182-7), are seen frequenting bars, cafés, *casas de citas* or, occasionally, at home. Although Marco appears only three times during the course of the chapter it is significant that one of these occasions is the only exterior scene in III (199-201). After his encounter with Ventura in the café on San Bernardo, Marco has continued his odyssey and is now seen gazing into a shop window (III, 200), as at the beginning of the second chapter. This time it is a *joyería* as opposed to the rather more mundane *tienda de lavabos*. There is a simple explanation as to why Marco apparently spends so much of his time wandering the streets —Pablo Alonso's condition

that he leave his room by 9.30 a.m. and not return before 11p.m.
(II, 141). On this particular occasion, the sight of Marco wandering
aimlessly serves as a prelude to Chapter IV, where he will be shown,
especially in the latter part, moving at night in an increasingly
frenzied manner through the near-deserted streets. Whilst most are
preparing for bed, the narrative shifts back and forth from bedrooms
to the streets where Marco roams, reluctant to go "home". Thus,
whereas Chapters I and III are composed almost totally of interior
scenes, Chapters II and IV, with Marco dominating a large part of
each, display a continual alternation between interior and exterior
events.

Chapter IV marks the first major movement back in time, from the
afternoon of the second day (Chapter III) to the night of the first
day. Accordingly, the new chapter might have been expected to
continue and develop events narrated in Chapter II. Yet although
the murder of doña Margot provided the hub of the last part of that
chapter, there is but a single, indirect reference to it in Chapter IV
and this comes from the author (IV, 225) and not from one of the
characters. With the exception of the *guardia*, Julio García Morrazo,
and a few others of minor importance, the characters encountered in
this chapter are already familiar. Victorita, the *novia* of the consumptive Paco, had been briefly seen in Chapter III. Now she emerges
with García Morrazo, Marco, and Roberto and Filo González to
dominate this nocturnal section of *La colmena*. García Morrazo
serves as the external point of reference for most of the chapter and
although presumably unacquainted with Marco, his structural counter-
part of the latter part of Chapter IV, is linked with him through
Celestino's bar and also the González's maid Petrita, who, it transpires,
is Morrazo's girl-friend.

Chapter V, set during the evening of the second day, is largely a
portrayal of the middle classes at play. Through the Moisés family it
shows a not untypical section of this stratum engaged in erotic
pursuits. As usual it is the pursuit that is shown rather than the
actual activity. However, whilst the affairs of Roque Moisés and his
daughter Julita dominate this part of the novel it is also made clear
that they are no more than victims of a general middle-class malaise
that results in the quest for erotic relief from the monotony of everyday life. Mario de la Vega reappears, this time in confrontation with

Victorita (V, 280-1) and perhaps most disturbing of all is the scene toward the close of the chapter where the doctor, Francisco Robles, hands a thirteen-year-old girl over to doña Celia for his future enjoyment (V, 328-9). The purpose of the telephone call from Robles to doña Celia (III, 193 and V, 292-3) is thus revealed. This scene also serves to anticipate Chapter VI —the morning of the second day— where, against the background of the awakening city, the author gives biographical sketches of several of the girls who work in the *prostíbulo* of doña Jesusa, the place where Martín Marco had found a bed for the night at the end of Chapter IV.

Chapter V had dealt primarily with the diversions of the bourgeoisie; now in Chapter VI there is a serious look at the histories of some girls who, through adverse circumstances, found themselves exploited and abandoned. Although a new day is beginning, events occurring later in that day have already been seen in Chapters III and V; therefore the main body of the novel ends with the start of a new day and new opportunities, and yet many of the events that take place later have already been recorded. The future that Chapter VI anticipates has passed in Chapters III and V. Accordingly, by the end of Chapter VI it would appear that the future has little more significance than the past and both are, the structure of the narrative implies, little more than a recurring present. Cela is therefore using a structural technique to emphasize certain thematic qualities and the most obvious of these —and this will be discussed under the general heading of "Themes"— is that of the monotonous and repetitious nature of the existence of the society portrayed in *La colmena*:

> La mañana, esa mañana eternamente repetida, juega un poco sin embargo, a cambiar la faz de la ciudad, ese sepulcro, esa cucaña, esa colmena . . . (VI, 343).

Structurally, the brief *Final*, with the narrative alternating between Marco, as he makes his way to the outskirts of the city, and a group of his acquaintances, may appear to be something of an afterthought. Various characters, including his sister Filo, Ventura Aguado, Celestino Ortiz and Roberto González wish to warn Marco that the authorities are trying to locate him. The reason for this is unstated and the reader can only speculate. What is more intriguing is that Cela, after apparently terminating the narrative at the end of Chapter VI, has chosen to reopen it but still without attempting to resolve any of the situations presented in the novel. In fact, the author is doing quite the opposite. He is presenting in the *Final* yet another situation, the cause of which, like the outcome, is unknown to the reader. Thus, from a dramatic point of view at least, the word "final" is really something of a misnomer. It is also ironic, for by leaving *La colmena* as an *oeuvre ouverte*, almost as an afterthought it would seem, Cela has deliberately ruptured the hermetic structure of the rest of the novel and left it to the reader to postulate a sequel to the *Final* and perhaps even a semblance of plot, so obviously lacking elsewhere. One thing is, however, certain: the addition of the *Final* to the main body of *La colmena*, preconceived or otherwise, directs the reader forward into the unknown and at the same time causes more than a cursory glance back at the rest of the novel in quest of dramatic or thematic significance, or of both.

Before commencing a discussion of the themes of the novel, it will
be useful to recall Cela's statement in the *Nota a la primera edición*:
"*La colmena*, . . . no es otra cosa que un pálido reflejo, que una
humilde sombra de la cotidiana, áspera, entrañable y dolorosa realidad" (957).   Critics have generally concurred with regard to the
nature of the reality displayed and the themes that emerge in the
novel.   Eugenio de Nora mentions "los aspectos más negativos de la
vida (la ausencia de caridad, la promiscuidad y abyección de las
relaciones sexuales, el mísero cálculo de los pobres seres obsesio-
nados por la ganancia indispensable al sustento, la maldad gratuita,
etc.)" (*8*, 77).   Paul Ilie indicates two fundamental themes and also
suggests their cause: "Las condiciones económicas de Madrid revelan
una gran desigualdad en la distribución de la riqueza, de la cual nacen
dos temas fundamentales en la novela: dinero y sexo" (*10*, 139).
Alonso Zamora Vicente recognizes hardship as a theme of *La colmena*
but feels that the people portrayed have it in their own power to
remedy the situation and are prevented from so doing by their
mediocrity and spiritual impoverishment (*15*, 52-3).   The aimlessness of the existence of most of those seen —and of Martín Marco in
particular— is, in the opinion of D. W. Foster, a theme which the
structure of the novel "is designed to emphasize" (*9*, 79).   Finally, a
theme stressed by José Ortega, and which stems from the temporal
aspect of *La colmena*, is the repetitive nature of the lives of those
encountered in the narrative: "La temporalidad en *La colmena* es el
elemento fundamental que envuelve y aprisiona a todos los personajes.
. . . Esto, lo temporal y repetitivo de la existencia, es lo que Cela
quiere mostrarnos con su 'maquinilla de fotógrafo' " (*13*, 115).
   The repetitive and monotonous existences of most of those present
are not, however, necessarily the result of financial hardship and the
obvious restrictions that this would impose.   Indeed, the atmosphere
of both monotony and lethargy that pervades Chapter I, where the
clientele of doña Rosa's café is shown to be predominantly bourgeois,
would support Zamora Vicente's contention that the problem is
spiritual rather than material.   Also, whilst sex, which D. W. McPheeters

has termed "the common denominator in *La colmena*" (*12*, 99), will
be seen to provide a temporary respite from a largely drab existence
for both wealthy and poor, it is an escape, as Nora points out, which
takes two different forms: "El sexo es, por una parte, la 'liberación'
única al alcance de estos seres cercados por la miseria, en confluencia
con el erotismo como diversión preferida y barata de los más o menos
privilegiados" (*8*, 77).

Monotony

Whilst the theme of monotony is particularly emphasized in the
opening chapter of *La colmena*, it also constitutes an important
aspect of the rest of the novel. At times, Cela makes his own
unequivocal statement:

> Detrás de los días vienen las noches, detrás de las noches vienen
> los días. El año tiene cuatro estaciones: primavera, verano, otoño,
> invierno. Hay verdades que se sienten dentro del cuerpo, como el
> hambre o las ganas de orinar (II, 121).

Here, the inexorable march of time is seen as a repetitive and monotonous process of physical discomfort. The main concern for the
hungry of *La colmena* is to obtain food and survive, whilst the
financially secure will often be seen in quest of distraction. However,
it should be realized that for both groups the principal challenge that
has to be faced is that presented by the phenomenon of *time*: either
time signalling the interval between a meal and subsequent hunger, or
time as the vacuum to be filled by distractions in order to alleviate
the monotony of a tedious existence, or both.

In the introduction to the first volume of his *Obra completa*, Cela
says of the phenomenon of time:

> El hombre pierde siempre la permanente batalla que el tiempo
> le presenta. El hombre es la víctima propiciatoria que los dioses
> ofrecen, en sacrificio, al tiempo insaciable y jamás clemente. El
> tiempo, en su lucha con el hombre, juega con él y, cuando se
> aburre, lo mata. O lo deja morir cortándole el chorro del tiempo.
> Pero en la pelea contra el tiempo, y aun sabiendo de antemano que
> seremos vencidos por él, a los hombres no nos cabe más postura
> que la de hacerle frente con decisión, darle cara y, pase lo que pase,
> no huirle. A lo hecho, pecho. Es la vieja ley que jamás falla, y el
> hombre debe morir matando o, al menos, defendiéndose. Al
> tiempo no lo matamos, cierto es, pero lo herimos. El tiempo, en
> su lidia con el hombre, tampoco, aunque lleve la mejor parte, sale

incólume y de rositas.[6]

There is, of course, nothing new or startling in this observation on man's invincible adversary. Nor is there any attempt to make even a fleeting examination of the nature, subjective or objective, of the phenomenon. Cela's statement is simply concerned with *man* and time; expressing the belief that man should at least face the challenge that time presents and, presumably, regard that challenge as a stimulus.

This statement is, then, primarily concerned with man's psychological attitude toward time rather than his ultimate physical impotence. Whilst death is inevitable, life or time does, at least, present man with a certain potential. Social or physical circumstances may, of course, limit or even prevent an exploration of this potential, as may the absence of volition. Robert Spires, in his study of temporal and tonal paradoxes in *La colmena*, comments that man "cannot escape the tragic imprisonment of the temporal order of nature" (*14*, 874). Yet Spires fails to stress that, in the case of this novel, most of the characters lack the ability to see that they are, with their attitudes, unwittingly reinforcing their psychological confinement. As Ilie points out: "El pesimismo inherente a la novela brota no tanto de la situación de pobreza como de la incapacidad de las personas para mejorarla o para ayudarse a sí mismas psicológicamente" (*10*, 148-9).

The Opening Chapter

In the opening chapter, the author evokes an atmosphere of lethargy and stagnation. One of the most disturbing features apparent here is the attitude of apathy and resignation ascribed to most of those present in doña Rosa's café: "Los clientes ven pasar a la dueña, casi sin mirarla ya, mientras piensan, vagamente, en ese mundo que, ¡ay!, no fue lo que pudo haber sido, en ese mundo en el que todo ha ido fallando poco a poco, sin que nadie se lo explicase, a lo mejor por una minucia insignificante" (I, 51) and, shortly afterwards: "Los clientes de los cafés son gentes que creen que las cosas pasan porque sí, que no merece la pena poner remedio a nada" (I, 52). This suggested collective malaise, associated with the theme of the

[6]*Obra completa*, tomo I. *Las tres primeras novelas* (Barcelona: Destino, 1962), p. 12.

monotony of existence, is then examined on an individual basis.
Jaime Arce is not untypical; he either displays an inability to think
or, at best, exhibits a vague curiosity but which apathy or lethargy,
or both, prevent him from pursuing to any depth: "Don Jaime no
solía pensar en su desdicha; en realidad, no solía pensar nunca en
nada. Miraba para los espejos y se decía: ¿quién habrá inventado los
espejos? . . . Don Jaime cambia de postura, se le estaba durmiendo
una pierna. ¡Qué misterioso es esto! Tas, tas; tas, tas; y así toda
la vida, día y noche, invierno y verano: el corazón" (I, 53). Seoane,
the café violinist who views the clients from a different perspective,
also prefers not to think and spends the working day mentally
anaesthetized: "Seoane mira vagamente para los clientes del café, y
no piensa en nada. Seoane es un hombre que prefiere no pensar; lo
que quiere es que el día pase corriendo, lo más de prisa posible, y a
otra cosa" (I, 105).

The torpor exhibited in Chapter I reflects a psychological or
spiritual exhaustion in those shown, as well as a concomitant sub-
mission to a monotonous and largely meaningless existence:

> Flota en el aire como un pesar que se va clavando en los
> corazones. Los corazones no duelen y pueden sufrir, hora tras
> hora, hasta toda una vida, sin que nadie sepamos nunca, demasiado
> a ciencia cierta, qué es lo que pasa (I, 60).

Therefore, while doña Rosa assails and intimidates her employees,
her clients have, for the most part, already been reduced to a state of
quiescence and numbness by some intangible force that is omni-
present and has been frighteningly effective.

Apart from the ejection of Marco or the incident of the fainting
poet, doña Rosa's tantrums provide most of the brief intervals of
diversion in the café. Distraction is at a premium for most of the
clients who, in any case, prefer the role of the observer to that of
participant. A rare exception is presented with the two children
playing trains. They, at least, are making a conscious effort to
relieve their boredom but in the process are becoming bored by these
very efforts:

> Son dos niños ordenancistas, consecuentes, dos niños que juegan
> al tren, aunque se aburren como ostras, porque se han propuesto
> divertirse y, para divertirse, se han propuesto, pase lo que pase,
> jugar al tren durante toda la tarde (I, 66).

In this particular incident, these two children illustrate a frustration that besets even the very young. However, in Chapter I and especially in the early part, past and present frustrations of various clients provide a degree of thematic unity. We are informed of, for example, the fruitless business ventures of Leonardo Meléndez and Jaime Arce; Isabel Montes's loss of her young son; José Rodríguez's lottery prize of a mere forty pesetas; Trinidad García Sobrino's thwarted ambition to become a *diputado* and the prostitute Elvira's latest unprofitable affair. Even doña Rosa gives the impression of being continually frustrated by her employees, whilst at the end of the chapter there is an indication that she too has suffered from the vagaries of fate, which may, of course, explain her excess of spleen:

> Suenan las nueve y media en el viejo reló de breves numeritos que brillan como si fueran de oro. El reló es un mueble casi suntuoso que se había traído de la exposición de París un marquesito tarambana y sin blanca que anduvo cortejando a doña Rosa, allá por el 905. El marquesito, que se llamaba Santiago y era grande de España, murió tísico en el Escorial, muy joven todavía, y el reló quedó posado sobre el mostrador del café, como para servir de recuerdo de unas horas que pasaron sin traer el hombre para doña Rosa y el comer caliente todos los días, para el muerto. ¡La vida! (I, 105).

The themes of monotony, apathy and frustration thus dominate the opening chapter of *La colmena*. Despite the very beginning of the narrative, when mention of the possible lesbian tendency of doña Rosa, her interest in financial matters and, also, the reference to Meléndez's considerable debt might suggest a particular thematic direction for the chapter, sex and money (and hardship) are far less in evidence than those themes previously indicated. Sexual relationships, more extensively treated in later parts of the novel, are scarcely and obliquely mentioned here. The treatment is more in the form of background information concerning, for example, the recent affair of Elvira with don Pablo, Consorcio López's past, or the present activities of doña Asunción's daughter. The only notable reference to sexual morality is in doña María's conversation with doña Pura (I, 93-4); they believe that promiscuity was launched with the advent of the swimming pool and is fostered by the cinemas.

Similarly, the problem of financial hardship is little in evidence. The clients are predominantly bourgeois and both evidence and implication of hardship are infrequently encountered in this early part of the novel. Elvira is one of the few examples in Chapter I of the less fortunate. She is currently having little success in her calling and lives "una vida perra, una vida que, bien mirado, ni merecería la pena vivirla" (I, 55). Toward the end of the chapter there occurs a sympathetic reminder of her indigence: "La señorita Elvira tiene un aire débil, enfermizo, casi vicioso. La pobre no come lo bastante para ser ni viciosa ni virtuosa" (I, 98). Apart from Eloy, who is impressed by Mario de la Vega's apparent affluence and who needs a job, Martín Marco appears as the most obvious case of financial hardship. His ejection from the café evokes mixed reactions from those who witness it, including an understandable sympathy from Elvira.

Hardship and sex, then, are minor themes in the opening chapter of *La colmena* but will be developed as the narrative unfurls; hardship in particular in Chapters II, IV and VI and sex in III, IV and V. Chapter I serves to introduce some of the principal characters in the novel and, more important, to present the fundamental theme of monotony and its causes and derivatives —aimlessness, apathy, frustration and stagnation.

The Development of Themes

As has been mentioned, when Marco is followed away from the café at the beginning of Chapter II, the reader is introduced to a new environment and new sets of people. Marco and these new groups serve to give a different perspective to the narration by means of their own distinctive circumstances and attitudes. Although Marco dominates most of the second chapter and, with his own predicament and social ideas, serves to emphasize the theme of hardship and inequality, the reader is not convinced of the gravity of the problems facing many of his fellows. It is rather through the introduction of certain characters and the disclosure of their particular problems that this theme is most graphically and convincingly presented. Also, although hardship and the struggle for survival are the motifs of most of Chapter II, their presence is recurrent rather than continuous, with a telling contrast often being made between the less fortunate and their more comfortable fellows. Thus, Marco's thoughts or statements on inequality (for example, II, 113-14) may suggest the existence of social problems, but only when narrative access is gained to those actually suffering and also to those who are unaffected and prospering, is the problem of hardship both bared and emphasized. There is, for example, a significant difference between the well-being of Pablo Alonso and the precarious position of Filo and Roberto González. Pablo is able to enjoy those luxuries available to the wealthier of this society whilst Roberto and Filo struggle to acquire the necessities of life: "Ella trabaja hasta caer rendida, con cinco niños pequeños y una criadita de dieciocho años para mirar por ellos, y él hace todas las horas extraordinarias que puede y donde se tercie" (II, 122). Roberto and Filo are two of the most obvious examples of hardship in Chapter II and both are patently aware of the reality of their situation and the nature of their responsibilities. Similarly, the six-year-old *gitanito*, who had stirred Roberto's conscience as another even less fortunate than himself (II, 112), manages to maintain a precarious existence by dint of his own efforts. Martín Marco, on the other hand, prefers to apply much of his effort to theorizing rather than to the more mundane task of supporting himself, and he relies heavily on the generosity of others for survival.

At times, Cela emphasizes the contrasting fortunes of his characters by skilful juxtaposition of the short sections that constitute each chapter of *La colmena*. An example of this occurs with the reappearance of Elvira in Chapter II. First, Marco and Filo are seen together, then Pablo Alonso and his girl-friend Laurita and, finally, Elvira and Leocadia:

—Coge esas dos pesetas.
—No. ¿Para qué? ¿A dónde voy yo con dos pesetas?
—También es verdad. Pero ya sabes, quien da lo que tiene . . .
—Ya sé.

—¿Te has encargado la ropa que te dije, Laurita?
—Sí, Pablo. El abrigo me queda muy bien, ya verás como te gusto.
Pablo Alonso sonríe con la sonrisa de buey benévolo del hombre que tiene las mujeres no por la cara, sino por la cartera. . .
Pablo se deja querer.
—Quisiera ser la chica más guapa de Madrid para gustarte siempre . . . ¡Tengo unos celos!

La castañera habla con una señorita. La señorita tiene las mejillas ajadas y los párpados enrojecidos, como de tenerlos enfermos.
— ¡Qué frío hace!
—Sí, hace una noche de perros. El mejor día me quedo pas-

madita igual que un gorrión.
   La señorita guarda en el bolso una peseta de castañas, la cena.
   —Hasta mañana, señora Leocadia.
   —Adiós, señorita Elvira, descansar (II, 124-5).

Here, not only is the financial situation of Marco and Alonso contra-
sted, but also the opposing fortunes of Laurita and Elvira, with the
prostitute's jaded appearance and meagre supper shown to be a world
apart from the material well-being of Laurita and her desire to be
"la chica más guapa de Madrid".   Pablo Alonso is also clothing
Marco —Filo's enquiry as to whether Martín is wearing "una camiseta
marcada P.A." (II, 126) brings this fact to light— and thus Alonso,
like the baker el Señor Ramón, is aware of the problems of some of
his acquaintances and responds with deeds.   Even Celestino Ortiz is
generous to Marco by allowing him credit, an idea which doña Rosa'
would no doubt have found unpalatable.   Indeed, it is noteworthy
that her sole appearance in Chapter II merely shows her concern that
Marco has been suitably dealt with for his default of payment (II, 110).

   Chapter III moves forward to the second day of the action and
marks a change of thematic emphasis.   Themes already developed are
not abandoned, but temporarily submerged.   Chapter III (and also
Chapter V) deal in particular with the response of the wealthier to
the problem of monotony.   Chapter I suggests that many have succumbed to the corrosive nature of this phenomenon; III (and V) show
an attempt to combat monotony through diversion, and this diversion
is frequently of an erotic nature.   With several notable exceptions
such as Marco, Elvira and Petrita, the characters of Chapter III are,
like those of Chapter I, predominantly bourgeois and the chapter
commences with a series of views of leisure-time activities in bars and
cafés.   The theme of hardship is rarely encountered and even Martín
Marco is temporarily wealthy, receiving money from two of his
former fellow students.   The only real example of hardship and
suffering in this part of the novel is Victorita who, although employed,
needs extra money to buy medicines for her consumptive *novio*.   To
this end she is prepared to prostitute herself and is about to be introduced to Mario de la Vega by doña Ramona (III, 194).

   By and large, however, the plight of Victorita and Celestino Ortiz's
immediate acceptance of Petrita's offer of herself stand as two of the
more vivid examples of the erotic theme in Chapter III.   Far less

dramatic is the introduction of Roque Moisés and mention of his present and previous affairs (III, 178), or the account of the first visit of Julita Moisés and Ventura Aguado to doña Celia's *casa de citas* (III, 203-5). Alfonsito, the messenger boy of doña Rosa's café, is also seen being briefed on both the message he will carry to a married woman and his contingency plan should her husband come to the door (III, 169-70). The passwords that the child must utter and respond to suggest a certain melodrama and humour and, in fact, several other amorous escapades in this chapter are treated in a generally humorous manner. Even the congregation of the neigh-bours of the murdered doña Margot, orchestrated by don Ibrahím, is accorded fairly frivolous treatment and culminates in a mention of Fernando Cazuela's discovery during the search for the murderer: "Cuando todos los vecinos buscaban al criminal por orden de don Ibrahím se encontró con el amigo de su mujer, que estaba escondido, muy acurrucado, en la cesta de la ropa sucia" (III, 186). Also, the scene presenting Marujita Ranero's sinister telephone call to Consorcio López, her former *novio* and father of her twins, is terminated on a humorous note as López, in his excitement, sweeps over a shelf of bottles and, not surprisingly, incurs the wrath of the formidable doña Rosa (III, 171 and 195). The only explicitly erotic episode in the chapter occurs when Petrita gives herself to Celestino Ortiz in payment for Marco's debt to the bar owner. Her sacrifice is akin to that of Victorita and probably even more selfless. Petrita has no thoughts of seeking a relationship with Marco who is, in any case, unaware of her feelings and will, presumably, remain ignorant of this particular action. One of the ironies of this episode is that while Petrita is asking Celestino if she is worth the twenty-two pesetas that Marco owes him (III, 172), Marco, with Ventura Aguado in another bar, is receiving twenty-two pesetas in change from a waiter (III, 174).

The sexual theme is very much in evidence in Chapter IV, the nocturnal section of the novel, but presents itself largely in terms of solace for those who have survived the rigours of yet another day and less in terms of bourgeois diversion. Thus Petrita, with the day's chores completed and despite her feelings for Marco, goes to her *guardia* Julio García Morrazo and, for a brief while, as they make love, enjoys a certain liberation from her work and environment. Similarly, Roberto and Filo, with the day's exertions over, are also able to escape into the comfort and warmth of the physical expression of their love. The love play of Pirula and Javier, two of the more fortunate, is rather more stylized, yet not without tenderness (IV, 238 and 252-3). Pirula, at present living in comfort, had formerly worked with Victorita but now their ways of life are in complete contrast —a contrast which the author emphasizes by juxtaposing comments on their respective situations:

> La señorita Pirula tiene un instinto conservador muy perspicaz, probablemente hará carrera. Desde luego, por ahora no puede quejarse: Javier la tiene como una reina, la quiere, la respeta . . .

> Victorita no pedía tanto. Victorita no pedía más que comer y seguir queriendo a su novio, si llegaba a curarse alguna vez (IV, 238).

Victorita is the outstanding example of suffering (primarily emotional) in Chapter IV. Her situation also indicates how the less fortunate may be exploited and reminds the reader of the essential helplessness of the "have nots" of this society in the face of exploitation by the "haves".

In a chapter where sexual relationships are the fundamental theme, the final irony occurs when Marco, after wandering through the streets of the city as others are going to bed, finally finds shelter for the night and, in the arms of the prostitute Pura, refuses any sexual contact (IV, 273). The night enshrouds the city and provides its people with a brief respite before the new day brings the inevitable problems:

> La noche se cierra, al filo de la una y media o de las dos de la madrugada, sobre el extraño corazón de la ciudad.
> Miles de hombres se duermen abrazados a sus mujeres sin pensar en el duro, en el cruel día que quizás les espere, agazapado como un gato montés, dentro de tan pocas horas (IV, 273).

And yet, when next seen (Chapter V), the "cruel día" is shown primarily in terms of bourgeois diversion —away from the cafés and bars where these people had previously been encountered and now in the *casas de citas* where they seek to alleviate the monotony of their largely uneventful existence.

The episode which dominates the fifth chapter is centred around the use by Roque Moisés and his mistress and also by Julita Moisés and Ventura Aguado of doña Celia's *casa de citas*. Up to the point at which the episode is related, each couple had been unaware of the other's use of the location, and this accounts for the main dramatic interest of the situation. The thematic significance is obvious, with two members of the same middle-class family engaged in erotic pursuits. In addition, the coincidence involved in the use by father and daughter of the same *casa de citas* is also thematically important. By frequently linking characters and places Cela is continually implying that the people of *La colmena*, although inhabitants of a large city, are really only able to move in small, interlocking circles. Thus a narrative or structural technique is employed to emphasize thematic qualities. The lack of chronological sequence in the novel emphasizes their temporal confinement whilst the geographical and personal connections indicate a physical one.

Although the affairs of Roque and Julita Moisés dominate Chapter V, they are not the only members of their class shown to be seeking erotic diversion. Mario de la Vega appears in confrontation with Victorita and perhaps most frightening of all is the scene in which Dr Francisco Robles hands over the young girl to doña Celia (V, 329). This brief yet poignant episode serves to anticipate Chapter VI —"La mañana"— where, against the background of the stirring city, the author gives biographical sketches of several of the girls of doña Jesusa's *prostíbulo*. The sexual theme of Chapter V is thus continued although now it is no longer a question of the antics of the bourgeoisie and their efforts to amuse themselves but rather a serious look at the exploitation of girls forced into prostitution. This final chapter ends the body of the novel on a heavily pessimistic note. The city and its people awaken to the new day but for the majority there is little hope of relief or solace, let alone achievement. Leading sterile and futile existences, these people have already been, and will continue to be, relentlessly assailed and exhausted by the apparently insurmountable problems facing them —with the main problem being that of time and existence itself:

> La mañana sube, poco a poco, trepando como un gusano por los corazones de los hombres y de las mujeres de la ciudad; golpeando, casi con mimo, sobre los mirares recién despiertos, esos mirares que jamás descubren horizontes nuevos, paisajes nuevos, nuevas decoraciones.
>
> La mañana, esa mañana eternamente repetida, juega un poco, sin embargo, a cambiar la faz de la ciudad, ese sepulcro, esa cucaña, esa colmena . . .

¡Que Dios nos coja confesados! (VI, 342-3).

Throughout the six chapters that constitute the main body of *La colmena*, various themes have been introduced and developed. The inactivity of the opening chapter is succeeded by the activity of struggle and diversion, depending largely on the social stratum portrayed. Whilst each chapter emphasizes particular themes, within these thematic phases other themes previously presented do recur. This thematic flexibility is facilitated by the very structure of the novel and by the fragmentation of the narrative. The lack of chronological sequence, and continual movement back and forth, serve to stress the monotonous and repetitious existences that these people experience and seem ill-equipped to challenge.

Apart from the occasional moments of humour, the tone of *La colmena* is strongly pessimistic. The problems of monotony, hardship, aimlessness and stagnation may often appear to have a short-term remedy, yet there is never any serious attempt and seldom any desire to seek permanent solutions. Even in the *Final*, as Martín Marco appears to display a welcome and overdue enlightenment, one cannot help but suspect that he lacks the capacity to channel his new-found enthusiasm into serious efforts and that he will soon revert to his already familiar attitudes and behaviour. In any case, Marco is hardly representative of the society portrayed in *La colmena* and thus his new awareness, genuine or otherwise, is relatively unimportant within the context of the rest of the novel. For the vast majority, portrayed as incapable either of economic improvement or of even appreciating their own stagnation, there seems to be precious little chance of material or spiritual salvation. They are trapped both psychologically and physically and there is no indication that they have, in their power, any remedy.

V Martín Marco

Of the many characters in *La colmena*, none is more important than
Martín Marco. Whilst he is the obvious hub of the action in the *Final*
he is also the character who appears with more frequency in the other
chapters and the one accorded the most intimate portrayal by Cela.
D. W. Foster has commented: "Martín is a novelistic expedient forced
by the structure of *La colmena*. When compared with the other
characters of the novel, nothing marks him as outstanding. He is one
among many who are alike in their problems and sufferings. His
activities are placed in relief solely for the purpose of establishing a
point of reference for the narrative and to provide a vertebra for a
novel which to many critics seems to be the invertebrate novel without
equal" (*9*, 80). J. M. Castellet expresses a similar view with regard to
Marco's role in the novel: "No es más que una figura simpática a la que
el autor utiliza como truco técnico para trazar con ella, con sus peri-
pecias, una línea-eje a ambos lados de la cual desplegará a los demás
personajes, que no deberán apartarse demasiado de ella" (*16*, 31).
These two views are not untypical of critical assessments of Marco's
importance in *La colmena*, indicating the tendency to regard him as
primarily a structural device, a unifying element in a novel whose main
structural characteristic is its extensive fragmentation. However,
whilst the technical importance of Martín Marco cannot be denied, it
is also evident that he is by far the most complex and most interesting
of the characters encountered in the novel. His portrayal as the underfed and dissatisfied intellectual, expounding (often in a rather confused manner) many of the problems and grievances that he sees in his
society, indicates that Cela's aim has been to create a central figure
of thematic significance and of interest in his own right, as much as a
mechanism of cohesive value to the novel.

Marco's Itinerary

Before embarking on a discussion of the character and importance
of Martín Marco, it will be useful to summarize where and when he
appears in the narrative and thus trace his movements from his first,
unobtrusive appearance in Chapter I, to the prominence that he enjoys

in the *Final*. Marco's mobility throughout *La colmena* clearly distinguishes him from his fellows and also (from a structural viewpoint) enables Cela to use him to link characters and locations. However, although Marco is seen more than any other character in the novel, he is far from being under constant surveillance. His progress is followed intermittently, with the reader frequently unaware of what he may be doing and where at any given time. Thus, for example, Marco's whereabouts between the time of his anticipated breakfast with Purita (VI, 342) and his meeting with Ventura Aguado during the late afternoon of the same day (III, 173-4), are unknown. Therefore, any attempt to trace Marco's movements throughout the novel must be made with the awareness that the author has left many intentional gaps in his surveillance.

Chapters I, II, IV and VI show Martín Marco's movements from his removal from doña Rosa's café during the evening of the first day (I, 73) to his getting out of bed at doña Jesusa's *prostíbulo* on the morning of the second day (VI, 342). Marco's progress from café to *prostíbulo* is fairly extensively covered, commencing with his identification at the beginning of Chapter II as "el hombre que no ha pagado el café" (II, 108). He is then followed intermittently as he makes his way through the streets to the Metro and thence to the flat of his sister, Filo González (II, 123). The narrative is then interspersed with several scenes between brother and sister, until Marco leaves Filo (II, 131) and is next seen arriving at Celestino Ortiz's bar (II, 136). When he leaves the bar and shortly afterward bumps into his friend Paco (II, 139), the time would be around midnight and, aptly, in the last section of the chapter in which Marco appears, the reader is informed: "Martín pasa las noches en casa de su amigo Pablo Alonso, en una cama turca puesta en el ropero" (II, 141).

Chapter IV sees Marco coming across la Uruguaya and her boyfriend and then joining them for a drink (IV, 232-3) before continuing his wanderings through the streets, "sin querer irse a la cama" (IV, 254). As he makes his way toward the *casas de citas* on Alcántara, Montesa and Naciones he is stopped and asked to produce his papers (IV, 260). Although he says that he does not have them with him, the policeman does not press him and bids Marco farewell in an amicable manner. Marco is next seen moving hurriedly through the streets in a confused and distressed state of mind (IV, 263-6). He eventually finds his way to doña Jesusa's *prostíbulo* and is finally seen going to bed with Purita at around 1.30 a.m. (IV, 273). Chapter VI, morning of the second day, begins with Marco awakening refreshed (VI, 331) and shows him twice more before he gets up to face the new day (VI, 342).

Chapters III and V are both set during the afternoon and evening of this second day and show Marco requesting and receiving money from two former fellow students, Ventura Aguado (III, 173-4) and Nati Robles (III, 215). He then decides to return to doña Rosa's café in order to give "una lección a esa tía asquerosa del café" (V, 307). Marco loses twenty-five pesetas in the café lavatory (V, 309) and then proceeds to Rómulo's bookshop to buy Nati a present, where he discovers the loss of the money (V, 328). Thus Chapters VI, III and V show Marco's declining fortunes during the second day of the action whereas I, II and IV had traced his ascending fortunes from his ejection from the café to the more generous treatment received at doña Jesusa's *prostíbulo*.

In the *Final* Marco is seen making his way to the cemetery on the outskirts of Madrid where his mother is buried. He spends a while at her graveside (*Final*, 354-5) and, as he leaves the cemetery, decides that the time has come to seek regular employment and organize himself generally (*Final*, 356-9). *La colmena* closes with Marco on his way back to the city centre, cheerfully engrossed in his plans for the future and oblivious of the fact that the authorities are looking for him and that many of his acquaintances are much concerned on his behalf. This final section of the novel is almost totally dominated by Marco. For the first time a sizeable and diverse group of people are preoccupied with the question of his whereabouts and, also for the first time, the attention of the narrative is continually focussed on Marco, during both his presence and his absence.

Marco's Character

Throughout the narrative, then, Martín Marco's actions are frequently observed. In the periods in which he does not figure in the account, the reader often attends those people who are in some way, either directly or indirectly, connected with him: his sister Filo and her family; Celestino Ortiz; Pablo Alonso and Laurita; Ventura

Aguado and Julita or doña Rosa and the clients of her café. Other
characters, not personally acquainted with Marco, share with him a
common bond: the city and its streets, cafés, *casas de citas* and bars
—in fact, the common property and experience of many of the people
of the Madrid of 1943.

In the opening chapter of *La colmena*, as the narrator presents the
various clients of doña Rosa's café, Marco becomes, for a short time,
the centre of attention. His failure to pay is brought momentarily
into narrative focus, as are the ensuing reactions of several of the
other clients. Although he is not identified at this stage, the reader is
given some biographical details, sarcastic in flavour, which suggest
that this man is not just another down-and-out:

> El hombre no es un cualquiera, no es uno de tantos, no es un hombre
> vulgar, un hombre del montón, un ser corriente y moliente; tiene
> un tatuaje en el brazo izquierdo y una cicatriz en la ingle. Ha
> hecho sus estudios y traduce algo el francés. Ha seguido con
> atención el ir y venir del movimiento intelectual y literario, y hay
> algunos folletones de El Sol[7] que todavía podría repetirlos casi de
> memoria. De mozo tuvo una novia suiza y compuso poesías
> ultraístas (I, 73).

Marco's shabby attire is noted during this brief glimpse of him in
Chapter I and also when he reappears at the beginning of II. But of
more interest on these occasions are the author's comments on the
state of mind suggested by the man's appearance: "triste y amarga la
mirada, preocupada y como sobrecogida la expresión . . . parece un
niño abandonado" (I, 71), and: "mira la ciudad como un niño enfermo y acosado" (II, 108).

Henceforth, Marco will be shown as an individual who sees himself in a hostile urban environment. He is seen initially as one of the
many "nave nots" of the Madrid of 1943, disgruntled not only with
his personal condition but also with that of the society around him.
He expresses egalitarian ideas —a hazardous tendency considering
the contemporary political climate and the Government's continued
harsh repression of known left-wing activists and sympathizers.
When Marco meets Nati Robles (III, 199), it is learned that, before
the Civil War, both were members of the F.U.E. —Federación

---

[7]An independent daily newspaper of liberal views, which was founded in 1916
and ceased publication in 1937. *El Sol* was, during its lifetime, the most
intellectual and best written Spanish newspaper.

Universitaria Escolar— a left-wing Students' Union. This fact may explain his reticence when he meets Nati or indeed anyone who might be acquainted with his activities before the Civil War.

In his portrayal of Marco, Cela pays a considerable amount of attention to the man's views on society. Marco's ideals, commendable as they may be, are often shown to be the end-product of not too carefully formulated thoughts and, at times, the result of emotion rather than reason. His intellectual self-esteem is also accompanied by a tendency to oversimplify issues. As Marco is followed across the city in Chapter II and expounds his thoughts on social injustice and inequality it is apparent that his aims, although generally sound in principle, would require drastic or ludicrous means to be achieved. Cela's first real look inside Marco's mind is lengthy, but worth quoting in full since it is also indicative of the author's attitude toward his main character:

—La vida —piensa— es esto. Con lo que unos se gastan para hacer sus necesidades a gusto, otros tendríamos para comer un año. ¡Está bueno! Las guerras deberían hacerse para que haya menos gentes que hagan sus necesidades a gusto y pueda comer el resto un poco mejor. Lo malo es que cualquiera sabe por qué, los intelectuales seguimos comiendo mal y haciendo nuestras cosas en los cafés. ¡Vaya por Dios!

A Martín Marco le preocupa el problema social. No tiene ideas muy claras sobre nada, pero le preocupa el problema social.

—Eso de que haya pobres y ricos —dice a veces— está mal; es mejor que seamos todos iguales, ni muy pobres ni muy ricos, todos un término medio. A la humanidad hay que reformarla. Debería nombrarse una comisión de sabios que se encargase de modificar la humanidad. Al principio se ocuparían de pequeñas cosas, enseñar el sistema métrico decimal a la gente, por ejemplo, y después, cuando se fuesen calentando, empezarían con las cosas más importantes y podrían hasta ordenar que se tirasen abajo las ciudades para hacerlas otra vez, todas iguales, con las calles bien rectas y calefacción en todas las casas. Resultaría un poco caro, pero en los bancos tiene que haber cuartos de sobra.

Una bocanada de frío cae por la calle de Manuel Silvela y a Martín le asalta la duda de que va pensando tonterías (II, 113-14).

Marco loves to hear his own thoughts or perorations, and despite the fact that he is, on this occasion, possibly conscious of his vitiating inconsistency, is seldom spared Cela's gentle mockery, thus suggesting that perhaps the man is not to be taken too seriously.

Unfortunately, Marco's utopian ideals do not keep him alive. He

has no fixed income but is a freelance writer, contributing to the
network of Falange publications. All articles written had to be sub-
mitted to the Vicesecretaría de Educación Popular in the Calle de
Génova and, if approved, were subsequently published in various
provincial newspapers of the Movimiento. In writing for the right-
wing press (the left-wing and liberal presses had, needless to say, dis-
appeared) Marco is probably showing a measure of expediency rather
than a taste for ideological duplicity. However, he does, from time to
time, betray a certain élitist facet of his character, particularly with
regard to his intellectual ability and responsibilities, and this makes his
participation in the Falange press a little more understandable. In any
case, at least Marco has an outlet for his creativity and one which
brings him a little money. He is proud of being a writer and readily
furnishes details of his work when he is asked in Chapter IV to produce
his papers. Marco is surprised that the policeman does not recognize
him and then proceeds to give the rather grandiose title of his latest
article:

A Martín le extraña que el policía no lo reconozca.
—Colaboro en la prensa del Movimiento, pueden ustedes pre-
guntar en la vicesecretaría, ahí en Génova. Mi último artículo
salió hace unos días en varios periódicos de provincias, en Odiel, de
Huelva; en Proa, de León; en Ofensiva, de Cuenca. Se llamaba
Razones de la permanencia espiritual de Isabel la Católica (IV,
261-2).

The occasional nature of this employment means than Marco
relies to a great extent on the generosity of others for his survival. His
sister Filo gives him food and a little money when she can afford to;
from Pablo Alonso he receives shelter and some clothing and, from
Celestino Ortiz, credit. Doña Jesusa, on one occasion at least, gives
him a bed for the night and Purita for company and, during the brief
period of the action, Marco requests and receives money from
Ventura Aguado (III, 173) and Nati Robles (III, 215). Yet, although
he is ever ready to take advantage of help offered, he is basically
very proud and resents compassion and charity and, even more, any
allusion to his dependence on others. In a conversation between
Marco and Filo, Pablo Alonso's vest and her husband's tobacco
illustrate, on the one hand, Marco's sensitivity and, on the other
hand, his willingness to take advantage of any source of comfort that
presents itself. The time of year is early December and Filo asks

her brother if he is wearing a vest:

　　—Pues claro que llevo camiseta.　¡Cualquiera anda por la calle sin camiseta!

　　—¿Una camiseta marcada P.A.?

　　—Una camiseta marcada como me da la gana.

　　—Perdona.

　　Martín acabó de liar un pitillo con tabaco de don Roberto.

　　—Estás perdonada, Filo.　No hables de tanta terneza.　Me revienta la compasión (II, 126).

Although Marco does not revere Nietzsche as overtly as Celestino Ortiz, he nevertheless concurs with the philosopher in his rejection of compassion and Cela later comments: "A Martín no le divierte la caridad.　En el fondo, Martín es también un nietzscheano" (IV, 271).

Marco, then, accepts assistance but deeply resents any reminder of his indigence and dependence on others.　When Celestino Ortiz mentions the money that Marco owes him, the latter, in a calculated display of hostility, counters with scorn and insults (II, 137-9).　Here Marco indulges, to a certain extent, in histrionics and demonstrates a similar tendency when he returns to doña Rosa's café with money received from Nati Robles.　On this occasion he is determined to show that he is not the vagrant that his previous failure to pay might have suggested.　In the café Marco acts flamboyantly and informs the startled waiter: "Yo no soy ningún muerto de hambre" (V, 308).　Ironically, he then drops twenty-five pesetas in the café lavatory, returns to his table, makes a couple of scathing comments and leaves, satisfied that he has made his point but still unaware of his loss (V, 309).　Thus Marco's proud and triumphant gesture is shown, in fact, to end in the worst possible kind of disaster for him.　A further irony occurs when Seoane, the café violinist, finds the money and uses it toward the cost of a badly needed pair of glasses for his wife (V, 314).　Marco's pride has, therefore, on this occasion at least, indirectly benefited one of his needy fellows.

In addition to his apparent disdain for the help or interest of others, Marco has developed something of a persecution complex. Whilst some live well, he must suffer "la miseria de los intelectuales" (II, 117).　However, Cela does suggest that the apprehension that Marco displays at times is not necessarily the product of his fear of persecution, political or otherwise, but may be caused by something as basic as hunger.　After being stopped by the policeman in Chapter

IV, Marco, distressed and debilitated, refers to his own hunger
(IV, 265) and the author reiterates the point on the occasion of his
meeting with Nati Robles:

> Martín la miró temeroso. Martín mira con cierto miedo a todas
> las caras que le resultan algo conocidas, pero que no llega a
> identificar. El hombre siempre piensa que se le van a echar encima
> y que le van a empezar a decir cosas desagradables; si comiese
> mejor probablemente no le pasaría eso (III, 200).

Thus, he sees himself as a victim, or potential victim, of others'
mistrust, selfishness and spite. He believes, for instance, that his
brother-in-law's hostility is responsible for their mutual dislike: "Yo
lo noto y me defiendo" (II, 128) and he is also prepared to accuse
friends and others of a similar hostility. Characteristic is Marco's
belief that, when he was removed from doña Rosa's café by Pepe,
the waiter was only too ready to use violence. Although the scene
between the two men suggests that the thought was furthest from
Pepe's mind (II, 107), Marco later implies no such possibility:

> —Hoy me echaron a patadas de otro café.
> —¿Te pegaron?
> —No, no me pegaron, pero la intención era bien clara (II, 140).

The overall impression gained of Marco is that of an underfed and
dissatisfied intellectual, both defensive and aggressive, prone to self-
pity and who assumes the role of conscience of his society. In *La
colmena*, deprivation is shown as a major phenomenon in this section
of 1943 Madrid society. Marco voices some of the obvious grievances
and stresses the inequality that exists, yet he fails, it seems, to see
the real tragedy —the loss of dignity, or even the degradation, of both
the relatively wealthy and the poor. The latter are often forced to
undergo privations and humiliation at the hands of those with money
and power. The abuse of this dominant position obviously suggests
that, at least in Cela's opinion, power generates corruption rather
than a sense of responsibility. Examples are numerous. Doña Rosa
and Mario de la Vega find the humiliation of others a pleasant pastime.
Victorita decides to sell herself in order to buy medicines for her
consumptive *novio* and is just one example of the plight of those
without money. Her actions may well ennoble her in the eyes of the
reader, but it is difficult to feel anything other than distaste for doña
Ramona, who procures her, and Vega, who is prepared to take
advantage of her unfortunate circumstances.

Hunger, degradation and lack of purpose are the salient character-
istics of this society and yet Martín Marco, the supposed thinker, is
basically too egotistical to see very much beyond "la miseria de los
intelectuales". He fails, for example, to appreciate the honest
struggle for survival of his sister Filo and her family, because he is
always too preoccupied with his own situation and petty hostilities.
The cause of the mutual hostility between Marco and his brother-in-
law Roberto is unknown. Marco's feelings may be connected with a
probable incestuous relationship or incident with his sister many
years before (IV, 269), or may be merely the product of distaste or
resentment inspired by Roberto's industry and parsimony. But,
whatever the reason, Marco scorns Roberto's practical approach to
life and pompously suggests the desirability of his own dogmatic
approach:

> Martín toma un ligero aire retórico, parece un profesor.
> —A él le es todo igual y piensa que lo mejor es ir tirando como
> se pueda. A mí, no; a mí no me es todo igual ni mucho menos. Yo
> sé que hay cosas buenas y cosas malas, cosas que se deben hacer
> y cosas que se deben evitar (II, 128-9).

Marco sees himself as an idealist and an intellectual and yet it is
difficult to view him seriously as such and far easier to become
impatient with his varying attitudes of arrogance, pomposity or
self-pity. He is reluctant to consider the causes of his present personal
predicament and, although often disdainful of help profferred, continues to lead a largely parasitic existence. Thus the principles of the
man and his pride are flexible, and adjustable to the exigencies of the
moment. When Marco states his concern with the prevalent social
injustice, there are grounds for suspecting, after some acquaintance
with him, that he may well be more preoccupied with the treatment
that he personally receives from his fellows, and with the benefits
that would accrue to him in an egalitarian society. Thus, his desires
for equality are probably not born of altruism and, in any case, he
may be thinking simply in terms of equality of the masses, controlled
by the intellectual élite —an élite which could constitute Marco's idea
of the Nietzschean aristocracy and of which he would, no doubt,
expect to be part.

Finally, and ironically, when Marco does decide to take hold of
himself and follow a more practical course of action, it seems as if it
is already too late. The unexplained events of the *Final* give rise to

speculation as to why Marco is being sought by the authorities. However, since there is no firm indication in the novel of what it is that Marco may have done, speculation is all that the reader is allowed. In *La colmena* Cela frequently presents potentially interesting situations and chooses not to bring them to a conclusion. Obviously, the brief time span of the action and the large number of characters involved tend to preclude a detailed examination of many situations, their development and resolution. The *Final*, where neither the cause of events nor the outcome is shown, is the most striking example in *La colmena* of Cela denying his reader complete access to information concerning an apparently important situation. Thus, the novel ends with an enigma to which Martín Marco presumably holds the key.

Whilst his friends and family make frantic efforts on his behalf, Marco wanders blissfully through the outskirts of the city, appearing at last to see things in some sort of perspective. Just how serious his intentions might be is impossible to ascertain and, in any case, his new attitude will not, presumably, be given the opportunity of being put to the test. Apart from deciding to get a regular job he also appears to have modified at least one of his ideas: he now recognizes, and this contrasts with his earlier, rather more casual, pronouncement (II, 113), that war is senseless, although as much from a cultural as a human standpoint:

—Esto de la guerra es la gran barbaridad. Todos pierden y ninguno hace avanzar ni un paso a la cultura (*Final*, 358).

Yet there is really scant evidence to suggest that Marco's professed change of heart implies a total re-examination and modification of his ideas and attitudes. His immediate intention is merely to find regular employment. This is certainly a step in the right direction and, if serious, marks a realization of the need to support himself rather than continue his precarious and apparently humiliating existence. Marco may have come to see that however bourgeois (and therefore degrading) regular work might be, it is probably more palatable than his present dependence on others. Thus, an appreciation of the immediate problems facing him is, at most, the extent of his enlightenment. To see the emergence of a drastic change of attitudes is, judging by what is known of Marco, fanciful. Indeed, it would not be ungenerous to regard his intention to find regular work as merely a whim to be forgotten by the next day. As he discusses the various employment possibilities, a certain levity is evident —giving the impression that Marco is simply playing with a new idea and enjoys hearing his thoughts:

Martín está encantado consigo mismo.
— ¡Hoy sí que estoy fresco y discurro bien! Debe ser el aire del campo (*Final*, 358).

Throughout the novel Marco has said enough and Cela has made ample comments to ensure that, although the man takes himself very seriously, those acquainted with him, including the reader, do not. Perhaps the real irony of the *Final* is that, for the first time, a few people, as well as the authorities, are taking Marco seriously and of this is he is completely unaware. Cela exploits the *Final*, and particularly that part that sees Marco with the newspaper containing his name in the *edictos*, to indulge in a few closing dramatic ironies. Thus, Marco sits down with his newspaper and thinks to himself:

—A veces, en la prensa, vienen indicaciones muy buenas para los que buscamos empleo (*Final*, 357),

and, shortly afterwards:

Se palpa el periódico y sonríe.
— ¡Aquí puede haber una pista! (*Final*, 359).

The author, who through his presentation of Marco has consistently suggested his own attitude as one of amusement and tolerance, can-not resist interjecting a final, sardonic comment before leaving Marco to go cheerfully rambling on his way:

—Hoy verán los míos que soy otro hombre.
Los suyos pensaban algo por el estilo (*Final*, 359).

The Importance of Marco

Martín Marco is, without doubt, the most important and most fascinating character to appear in *La colmena*. His structural import-ance is twofold. First, owing to his almost constant mobility in the novel, he is —much more than any other single character— a means of linking many of the people and places presented in the narrative. Second, his recurring presence does give a measure of structural cohesion to the fragmented narrative, whilst his mobility helps create an impression of narrative progress where, in fact, there is little. Yet, despite this, it would be an error to regard Marco as indispensable to the structure of *La colmena*, or to assume that the structure has been designed around him. Foster's comment that Marco is "a novelistic expedient forced by the structure of *La colmena*" (9, 80) is preceded by: "The essential aimlessness of his existence stands out vividly. The structure of *La colmena* is designed to emphasize this aimlessness" (9, 79). Which came first, the structure of the novel or Marco's aimlessness? I think that the answer to this question is that Cela probably saw Marco as structurally useful, a way of giving some loose form of cohesion to his narrative and at the same time providing a recurrent dramatic focus for the reader.

As a character study, Marco is unique in the novel in that he receives a significantly more profound and extensive treatment from Cela than any of his fellows. It is relatively easy to categorize most of the other characters as malicious, honest, pathetic, arrogant, sympathetic, etc., as their most salient traits are displayed, and the reader is rarely given grounds for modifying the initial impression received. Marco, however, is accorded a portrayal that constantly reveals some new facet of his character or explores in greater depth one already disclosed. He is shown to be arrogant, pathetic, parasitic, proud, sensitive, and several other things, and the author often returns to explore a particular aspect of his qualities, good or bad. All in all, he is basically egotistical and inadequate. One may sympathize with his predicament for a time but soon he tries the patience not only of many of his acquaintances but also of the reader. His theorizing on what he sees as the prevalent social ills of his society does not, by any token, convince the reader of the unfortunate plight of many of his fellows, for although Marco does, through his thoughts and perorations, introduce the themes of hardship and inequality, his ideas are often so badly formulated as to provoke impatience or a wry smile from both reader and author. Marco loves to play with his thoughts and words but fails to channel the intelligence with which he credits himself into a practical course of action. Most of Marco's fellows have the insight to realize that the immediate problem of survival centres around the empty stomach or an essential medicine —in fact, money and its acquisition. Marco, on the other hand, does not seem to arrive at this conclusion until the *Final* and even at this point it is easy, in view of his previous actions and attitudes, to be sceptical.

VI Some other characters

The second edition of *La colmena* contains a *Censo de personajes* compiled by José Manuel Caballero Bonald and which lists, according to a "Nota del Editor", "doscientos noventa y seis personajes imaginarios y cincuenta personajes reales; en total, trescientos cuarenta y seis" (958). The *Censo* is included in subsequent editions of the novel, up to and including the seventh, and then reappears in the tenth and eleventh editions but is omitted from the twelfth, that of the *Obra completa*. It is comprehensive, useful to the reader with its thumbnail sketches and also shows that Cela greatly underestimated, in his *Nota a la primera edición*, the number of characters appearing in *La colmena*. Unfortunately, the figure of 296, or the more comfortably rounded 300, has often been accepted as a numerical assessment of the character portrayals in the novel and, by extrapolation, a means of positing general conclusions with regard to both structure and characterization. Robert Kirsner writes: "There is not a single character, of the more than three hundred who appear in this work, who evokes unmixed horror" (*11*, 59). Juan Luis Alborg sees the work as "una novela de composición sinfónica, sin protagonistas ni personajes destacados, exactamente como una orquesta, ninguno de cuyos elementos es superior a los demás —aunque meta más o menos ruido—, pues todos juntos contribuyen por igual" (*6*, 95) and later comments: "*La colmena* nos sabe a poco, porque ninguno de sus personajes se detiene lo bastante para que podamos agarrarlo un poco e intimar con él" (*6*, 97). But most provocative of all is Arturo Torres-Ríoseco:

> En *La colmena* no hay estructura, ni tema, ni desarrollo anecdótico o psicológico: sólo hay bosquejos, incidentes, diálogos interrumpidos. Los personajes aparecen como si fueran formas mecánicas, objetivamente, en acciones rápidas. Permanecen así, fríamente incompletos, como personajes de una película. Yo diría que la técnica de Cela en esta novela es afortunada — ¡y también el lector!—, ya que si desarrollara cada personaje la obra tendría en vez de trescientas cincuenta páginas, cien mil (*16*, 68).

Fortunately, several critics have perceived that the characters appearing in *La colmena* have been subjected to varying degrees of both exposure and examination. Thus, Eugenio de Nora accepts the numerical accuracy of the *Censo* but then offers some realistic qualifications. The figures of 296 and 50 are:

> . . . cifras exactas como índice de nombres, pero evidentemente exageradas en cuanto a verdadera "creación" o captación de seres. Por mi parte, después de dos lecturas atentas, retenía la figura de unos 45 tipos, junto con unas cuantas anécdotas más bien desligadas de sus protagonistas. No creo que pueda pedirse más a un texto de 250 páginas (*8*, 76).

However, even to accept Nora's figure as the basis for a study of the principal figures would involve a lengthy undertaking and I therefore intend to restrict myself to a discussion of some twenty characters. This will concentrate on characters of major dramatic or thematic significance, or both. Also, it is important to include several characters of apparently minor significance who, despite their rare appearances in the narrative, impress themselves upon the reader and in so doing illustrate Cela's skill as a writer capable of both terseness and impact.

Entrepreneurs

Considering the extent to which much of the action of *La colmena* takes place in cafés, bars and *casas de citas*, it is not surprising that Cela should include and describe several characters who are the embodiment of small-scale free enterprise in post-war Madrid. The businesses involved here range from the patently successful, such as doña Rosa's café and el señor Ramón's bakery, to Leocadia's humble chestnut stall. Catering to a different kind of appetite are doña Celia's *casa de citas* and doña Jesusa's *prostíbulo*. Other proprietors include Mario de la Vega, Celestino Ortiz and doña Ramona who, along with those previously mentioned, receive a varying degree of attention and are shown to possess and exhibit distinctively different attitudes toward their fellows.

The most striking and formidable of these entrepreneurs is without doubt doña Rosa, owner of the café "La Delicia". Her café is the setting for the opening chapter and her presence dominates this early part of the novel. She directs a continual stream of abuse at her waiters, seizing upon any indication of a lack of thrift or diligence on their part as a justification for abuse and intimidation. Doña Rosa is a businesswoman and not a diplomat. She is intensely preoccupied with efficiency and profits, and forever eager to assert the power that

she enjoys. Gross in both comportment and aspect, she is also shown
to possess a nature as disagreeable as her outward appearance:

> Doña Rosa tiene la cara llena de manchas, parece que está siempre
> mudando la piel como un lagarto. Cuando está pensativa, se
> distrae y se saca virutas de la cara, largas a veces como tiras de
> serpentinas. Después vuelve a la realidad y se pasea otra vez, para
> arriba y para abajo, sonriendo a los clientes, a los que odia en el
> fondo, con sus dientecillos renegridos, llenos de basura (I, 50).

Despite a purported interest in the well-being of, among others,
Elvira, Seoane or his wife Sonsoles and despite her pronouncement:
"Aquí estamos para ayudarnos unos a otros" (I, 95), doña Rosa
shows scant concern for the predicament of her fellows: "El mundo
es su café, y alrededor de su café, todo lo demás" (I, 49). Thus when
Martín Marco violates the law of the café he is dealt with speedily and
decisively (I, 72). Don Roque Moisés, doña Rosa's brother-in-law,
also violates her code; his disregard for both the work ethic and
conventional moral norms is proclaimed and condemned (I, 59 and
97). However, some would say that even doña Rosa may not be
entirely free of moral turpitude, although considering her overriding
concern with money, the author hastens to express his own doubts
on this:

> Hay quien dice que a doña Rosa le brillan los ojillos cuando viene
> la primavera y las muchachas empiezan a andar de manga corta.
> Yo creo que todo eso son habladurías: doña Rosa no hubiera
> soltado jamás un buen amadeo de plata por nada de este mundo
> (I, 49).

For doña Rosa her café is much more than a means of acquiring
wealth, it is a monument to her successful commercial endeavours
and a symbol of her power:

> —Pero quien manda aquí soy yo, ¡mal que os pese! Si quiero
> me echo otra copa y no tengo que dar cuenta a nadie. Y si me da
> la gana, tiro la botella contra un espejo. No lo hago porque no
> quiero. Y si quiero, echo el cierre para siempre y aquí no se
> despacha un café ni a Dios. Todo esto es mío, mi trabajo me
> costó levantarlo.
>
> Doña Rosa, por la mañana temprano, siente que el café es más
> suyo que nunca.
> —El café es como el gato, sólo que más grande. Como el gato
> es mío, si me da la gana le doy morcilla o lo mato a palos (VI, 340).

Yet doña Rosa's obsession with her café and all that it represents is
not so all-consuming as to prevent an awareness of any indirect

menace to her position. She is, not surprisingly, an advocate of
public law and order (I, 100), and is also somewhat anxious concerning the progress of the Second World War. Her sympathies are for
the Germans and with the tide of battle turning against them, she
sees the European situation as a cause or reflection of "lo inseguro de
los tiempos" (VI, 340). Doña Rosa's association between the fortunes
of her establishment and those of Nazi Germany is, to an extent,
understandable:

> A doña Rosa le preocupa la suerte de las armas alemanas. Lee
> con toda atención, día a día, el parte del cuartel general del
> Führer, y relaciona, por una serie de vagos presentimientos que
> no se atreve a intentar ver claros, el destino de la Wehrmacht con
> el destino de su café (I, 103).

In view of the prevalent Spanish hostility toward communism and
fear of Soviet Russia and the long-lasting feeling amongst many of
the vanquishers of the Axis powers that Franco should be removed,
doña Rosa's apprehension is by no means groundless. Moreover,
she has far more to lose than most of her fellows.

After the first chapter, doña Rosa and her café are seldom
revisited. Other proprietors appear, but none is accorded as extensive
a portrayal and none is shown to be cast from quite the same mould.
Doña Rosa is Cela's *tour de force* in the novel, with no other character
matching her in sheer dramatic presence and imperiousness. Even
Marco, although more interesting and important, is a lightweight by
comparison and it is perhaps ironic that when doña Rosa has him
summarily dispatched from her café she is propelling him into
narrative prominence.

Two other successful entrepreneurs are the printer Mario de la
Vega and doña Ramona Bragado, owner of a *lechería*. However,
neither appears a paragon of commercial achievement. Instead, both
are shown primarily as exploiters of others' misfortune, Vega for
pleasure and doña Ramona for profit.

Vega is seen in Chapters I and II in the company of the unemployed
Eloy; he enjoys a little callous humour at the lad's expense and then
offers him a job. The printer is a self-made man who has achieved
success by dint of hard work and he so informs Eloy (I, 91-2). Later,
Vega buys Eloy supper, reveals his paternalistic attitude toward his
employees and then adds that Eloy will receive no contract in his
new job (II, 145-7). During this conversation Vega telephones, it

later transpires (IV, 222), doña Ramona. The subject of this call, although unnamed, is Victorita.

Doña Ramona's business acumen, as well as her principal sideline, is indicated when she is first encountered:

> . . . se dedicaba a todo lo que apareciese y era capaz de sacar pesetas de debajo de los adoquines; uno de los comercios que mejor se le daba era el andar siempre de trapichera y de corre-veidile, detrás del telón de la lechería (III, 163-4).

At this particular time she is engaged in procuring Victorita for Vega and the remainder of her appearances are centred around this enterprise. Similarly, after bidding goodnight to Eloy (IV, 260), Vega's impending arrangement with Victorita accounts for his subsequent narrative importance. In confrontation with the girl on the following day, Vega is touched by her obvious distress but is also practical enough to suggest that she go through with their projected liaison (V, 280-1). Victorita's ailing *novio* is, in fact, the brother of Eloy and it is ironic that Vega will come to the aid of both brothers, with a job for one and payment to Victorita that will enable her to buy medicines for the other. Thus doña Ramona and Vega, both successful in their respective businesses, are most strikingly shown as exploiters of a girl's desire to help her consumptive *novio*.

By way of contrast, Celestino Ortiz, who had fought in the Civil War under the Anarchist leader Cipriano Mera and who now owns the small bar "Aurora" and loves to study Nietzsche's work of the same name, is presented in a fairly humorous manner and in a far more sympathetic light. Ortiz lacks the commercial expertise of doña Rosa or doña Ramona and when, for example, he tries to obtain payment from Marco, extracts a barrage of abuse but no money, Later, when Petrita offers herself in settlement of this debt, he seems momentarily surprised, whilst in accepting her proposition he displays a spontaneous preference for pleasure over profits (III, 172).

Ortiz has a predilection for both reading and quoting from *Aurora* whilst at the same time feeling that "Nietzsche es realmente algo muy peligroso" (II, 135). In one scene, as he dreams of military valour, he is awakened by the mundane necessity to urinate and it is this kind of presentation that projects Ortiz as a slightly comical and amiable figure. Although he sleeps in his bar "porque le sale más barato y porque así evita que lo desvalijen la noche menos pensada"

(IV, 234), he is, unlike some of his peers, far from being obsessed with money. Ortiz is merely protecting his livelihood and in any case seems to prefer to use his bar more as a pulpit than a means of pursuing wealth.

An even more sympathetic portrayal is accorded doña Celia and doña Jesusa. They run, respectively, a *casa de citas* and a *prostíbulo* and thus their principal commercial concern is with catering to those intent on gratifying their sexual appetite. Both are presented as amiable and considerate and basically anxious to provide their clients with the best possible service. The Spartan simplicity of doña Celia's rooms is adequately compensated for by her treatment of the customers "con buena voluntad, con discreción y con mucho deseo de agradar y de servir" (III, 203), and she asks only that her discretion be reciprocated for the sake of the children. She becomes attached to her clients: "Es una dueña de casa de citas muy sentimental" (III, 213), and is prepared to protect them regardless of economic considerations. Thus she warns Ventura Aguado that Julita's father is one of her clients (V, 285), thereby attempting, as much for Julita's sake as her own, to avoid undesirable consequences.

Doña Jesusa is shown in an equally favourable light, both as an individual and as a business woman. Whilst her generosity toward Martín Marco is no doubt partly a result of her friendship with his mother, it is also clear that she tends the welfare of employee and customer alike and maintains a clean and well-organized establishment:

> En casa de doña Jesusa se lava la ropa de cama todos los días; cada cama tiene dos juegos completos que, a veces, cuando algún cliente les hace, incluso a propósito, que de todo hay, algún jirón, se repasan con todo cuidado (VI, 332).

Doña Jesusa makes only a handful of appearances in *La colmena* yet emerges as an honest and compassionate figure and both she and doña Celia are shown to be basically estimable individuals who stand in marked contrast to some of the wealthier and superficially more respectable entrepreneurs of their society.

Finally, a character who is commercially successful and who at the same time has retained his generosity and humanity, is the baker el Señor Ramón. He is introduced as "un hombre de buena sangre, un hombre honrado que hace sus estraperlos, como cada hijo de vecino, pero que no tiene hiel en el cuerpo" (II, 108). Ramón is generous with Roberto González, his part-time accountant, and is reproached by his wife for this and other examples of helping those in need (IV, 247). His business is the product of many years of self-sacrifice and dedication and, in consonance with his Spartan ways, Ramón enjoys the fruits of his success in a very modest fashion:

> El señor Ramón es hombre fuerte y duro, hombre que come de recio, que no coge catarros, que bebe sus copas, que juega al dominó, que pellizca en las nalgas a las criadas de servir, que madruga al alba, que trabajó toda su vida (VI, 338).

Ramón is conscious of his wife's disapproval of his generosity and seeks to avoid her awareness of it rather than change the habit. It is characteristic that, in the *Final*, he should offer to hide Martín Marco for a few days. When he informs González: "Aquí estamos todos para ayudarnos como buenos amigos" (*Final*, 352), he echoes a sentiment expressed earlier by doña Rosa (I, 95); in Ramón's case, however, there is no doubt of the sincerity of the statement. El señor Ramón is the outstanding example in *La colmena* of a character who has achieved and maintained commercial success without becoming obsessed with the profit motive and one who is also prepared to help those less fortunate than himself. As a result, the shabbiness of some of his commercial peers is emphasized and shown to be even more reprehensible than might otherwise be the case.

The Bourgeoisie at Leisure

The people who frequent the bars and cafés of *La colmena* are predominantly middle or lower-middle class and they are largely seen whiling away what seems to be an inordinate and overwhelming amount of free time. Whilst the more adventurous dedicate themselves to erotic pursuits, the vast majority are content to gossip, observe, comment or simply day-dream as they fidget at their café tables. Nowhere is this more apparent than in the opening chapter as Cela displays a varied group of some twenty customers engaged in a common activity —that of killing time.

Here, for example, the reader encounters Leonardo Meléndez, a pretentious and pompous character who delights in mentioning the former glories of his family: "Tiene aires de gran señor y un aplomo inmenso" (I, 50) yet who, somewhat incongruously, cadges cigarettes and owes the café bootblack six thousand *duros*. However, his financial straits and dependence on others do not prevent him from cultivating a veneer of superiority. He treats his creditors with scorn and even inspires feelings of admiration in the bootblack who is consistently unpaid for his professional services. Meléndez's achievement is that he manages to remain aloof from day-to-day money matters and at the same time exercises a certain fascination over those he exploits: "Don Leonardo es lo bastante ruin para levantar oleadas de admiración entre los imbéciles" (I, 100).

Jaime Arce is presented as a failed businessman who also maintains an air of importance but lacks Meléndez's calculating nature and who passively and harmlessly thinks the day away: "Ahora anda buscando un destino, pero no lo encuentra . . . se pasaba el día en el café, con la cabeza apoyada en el respaldo de peluche, mirando para los dorados del techo" (I, 53). His mental activity is largely confined to wondering how many consumptives there might be present in the café, practising his multiplication or reciting the names of the Visigothic kings of Spain. Arce's inertia, although more pronounced than that of many of his fellows, is symptomatic of a lethargic bourgeois mentality that seems to abound at the tables of doña Rosa's café.

A client who has, at least, achieved financial success is the money-lender Trinidad García Sobrino. Unfortunately, after much expenditure of time and money, he failed to realize his political ambition to become a *diputado* and now devotes himself to his lucrative business and spends his afternoons in the café with his grandson, "oyendo la música o leyendo el periódico, sin meterse con nadie" (I, 61). In contrast to Meléndez and Arce, Sobrino appears as one of doña Rosa's wealthier clients who regards her café as a place to enjoy a little time away from the chores of business rather than as a venue where empty pretensions may be aired with impunity. The café clientele is primarily shown to be a group of people indulging in a variety of insignificant conversations, pretentious and grandiose postures, mischievous thoughts and gossip, and who are generally illustrative of a segment of society with ample free time but precious little inclination to spend it in a more stimulating way, or any idea of how to do this.

Pablo Alonso has no such problems. He is described as "un muchacho joven, con cierto aire deportivo de moderno hombre de negocios" (II, 118) who is seen to enjoy the fruits of his moderate affluence. For Alonso, intent on impressing Laurita, his latest conquest, money is a commodity unworthy of direct mention although he is never reluctant to show that he has sufficient to obtain those luxuries denied to others. Thus a waiter can find Alonso some whiskey after being instructed: "Di en el mostrador que es para mí" (II, 118), and Alonso can also afford to clothe Laurita and enjoy showing his satisfaction at her gratitude and admiration: "Pablo Alonso sonríe con la sonrisa de buey benévolo del hombre que tiene las mujeres no por la cara, sino por la cartera" (II, 124). Martín Marco is another who relies on Alonso for shelter and cast-off clothing and, despite the fact that certain conditions are imposed on Marco, there is little doubt that Alonso feels an affection for him (II, 119). However, for all his charm and resources, Alonso is afflicted by the same lack of purpose and boredom that pervades many of his fellows. He is rapidly tiring of Laurita, owing mainly to her petty jealousies and generally uninspiring company (III, 167) and one can safely assume that Alonso will soon be employing his ostentatious generosity to find her successor.

The quest of the bourgeoisie for erotic diversion is, however, most fully explored with the presentation of the activities of Roque Moisés, his daughter Julita and Ventura Aguado. The dramatic irony resulting from the fact that Roque and his daughter and their respective partners use doña Celia's *casa de citas*, and also that Ventura has slept with Roque's mistress Lola (V, 311), is of less importance than the attitudes shown by the principals. As with Pablo Alonso, these characters are motivated as much by a desire for diversion as by an urge to fulfil emotional or even physical needs.

Roque Moisés's waywardness is proclaimed by his sister-in-law doña Rosa in Chapter I (59 and 97), and when he is first encountered it is learned that he not only reciprocates Rosa's animosity but also looks forward to the day when her café might belong to his daughters (III, 162-3). In the meantime he continues his comfortable existence, enjoying a regular game of dominoes, gently mocking his wife's eccentricities —"Cada día que pasa más convencido de que su mujer es tonta" (III, 177)—, and managing to conduct an affair with doña Matilde's *criada* Lola. Josefa, his previous paramour, had borne him three children and was eventually supplanted by her younger sister,

Lola. Roque is thus a practised philanderer who even consults his playing-cards for some indication of his future sexual fortunes (III, 178). What his cards do not foretell is that his eldest daughter is enjoying her own affair at doña Celia's and when he becomes aware of this fact it is sufficiently perturbing to dampen his sexual ardour, at least temporarily (V, 315).

Julita is introduced as "muy enamoriscada de un opositor a notarías que le tiene sorbida la sesera" (III, 189) and has clearly inherited her father's predilection for the pleasures of the flesh. Her relationship with Ventura Aguado is erotic rather than emotional and there is never any expression or indication of deep affection between the two. Indeed, the extent of Julita's affection for Ventura appears to be an admiration of his sexual appetite and prowess. She records their sexual performances in what amounts to an erotic log-book —a far cry from the more traditional romantic diary— and, despite momentary misgivings, is thoroughly captivated by her roguish *novio*:

> Sin embargo — ¡lo que son las cosas! — cuando va a salir de la alcoba, un chorro de optimismo le riega el alma.
> — ¡Es tan cachondo este repajolero catalán! (V, 307).

Julita does not, understandably, inform her mother of the nature of the relationship with Ventura and allows doña Visitación to indulge in typical maternal fantasies, even to the extent of envisaging a future grandson as a member of the priesthood. Julita, having previously described the high character of her *novio*, crowns her mother's contentment with the ironic statement: "—Yo creo que conocer a Ventura— los oídos de la muchacha zumban ligeramente— ha sido una gran suerte para mí" (V, 324).

Ventura Aguado is constrained to deceive his father in different matters. After already spending seven years attempting to qualify as a notary, Ventura is anxious to ensure the continuation of financial support from his father. Although he informs Martín Marco: "Ahora mi padre ha tirado de la cuerda" (III, 174), there is no real evidence of this. Indeed, the later comment: "Ventura Aguado Sans hace lo que quiere de su padre" (III, 191) suggests that Ventura will continue to receive money from his father and use it for the pursuit of pleasure. His principal recreation is his affair with Julita and his most regular expense is the price of a room at doña Celia's *casa de citas.* Ventura sees himself as a master of the art of seduction and proudly recounts his version of the conquest of Julita to the frustrated don Tesifonte: "La conocí en el Barceló el veintitantos de agosto pasado y, a la semana escasa, el día de mi cumpleaños, ¡zas, al catre!" (V, 313). A rather more mischievous facet of Ventura's character is indicated when he sends the photograph of don Obdulio with an anonymous note to Roque Moisés (V, 285-6). His only saving grace appears to be a concern for his friend and former fellow student Martín Marco. When Marco asks Ventura for money the latter gives more than the amount requested and in the *Final* both Ventura and Julita are among those seeking to locate and help Marco. These isolated displays of generosity and concern by no means indicate a "rake's reform" but merely suggest that Ventura is a knave with some redeeming features. As such he is not alone among the bourgeoisie seen in *La colmena* although he is certainly more successful than most in his pursuit of erotic recreation.

The Struggle for Survival

As the bourgeoisie of *La colmena* lead their comfortable but often monotonous existences a group of people are shown to be more concerned with survival itself. Pablo Alonso states that Martín Marco is experiencing "una mala temporada" (II, 119), yet Marco is at least able to obtain assistance from some of his more fortunate acquaintances. The same cannot be said of several others whose survival depends largely upon the success or failure of their own efforts. Such individuals are concerned with ensuring that they have the money to pay for the next meal rather than how they will while away the time between one meal and another.

The most obvious examples of this struggle for survival are Roberto González and his wife Filo, a couple whose rigorous existence stands in marked contrast to that of the doña Ramonas or Ventura Aguados of their society:

> Ella trabaja hasta caer rendida, con cinco niños pequeños y una criadita de dieciocho años para mirar por ellos, y él hace todas las horas extraordinarias que puede y donde se tercie (II, 122).

Thus, in addition to his regular employment, Roberto is constrained to take on all the part-time jobs he can find and often walks to his many jobs so as to reduce his expenses. Although she can ill afford

it, Filo gives money and food to her brother Martín Marco and both
she and Roberto still manage to recognize that they are, in fact, more
fortunate than some. Roberto's " ¡Mientras todos tengamos salud! "
(IV, 262) and his wife's " ¡Cuántos están peor!" (IV, 263) may sound
somewhat hackneyed, yet they are sincere expressions of gratitude
that their own plight is less than it could be. At least they are
managing, for the moment, to make ends meet. The hardships that
they experience also appear to bring them closer together. They are
one of the few couples in *La colmena* who express and demonstrate
mutual affection and they are even prepared to run the risk of
having yet another mouth to feed (IV, 266-7).

Whilst sound health is one of the few blessings that Roberto and
Filo enjoy, the attitudes and behaviour of Victorita are determined
by her desire to see her *novio* cured of consumption. She firmly
believes that with sufficient nourishment and medicines Paco can be
cured, thereby assuring their future happiness. Victorita is prepared
to sell her services out of love and desperation and, as a result of her
straits, has learned to practise fortitude but also exhibits a spirited
aggression when confronted with either her callous mother or those
who would capitalize on her predicament.   Despite her sexual
appetite, which she freely admits to Paco, Victorita has resisted
previous desires to sleep with men other than her *novio* and reluctant-
ly takes the decision to prostitute herself: "Victorita no sentía deseos
ningunos de golfear; pero a la fuerza ahorcan" (IV, 238). She has not
slept with Paco for close on four months and finds herself in a
position where she must sleep with other men in order to save the
man she loves. Only in this way can she hope to resume the one
physical relationship that is important to her. In view of her plight
one can easily excuse the fury that she occasionally unleashes and
sympathize with her as, for example, she addresses Mario de la Vega
with a frankness and resignation that is indicative of her emotional
exhaustion:

> Yo quiero mucho a mi novio. A usted nunca lo querré, pero en
> cuanto usted me pague me voy a la cama. Estoy muy harta. Mi
> novio se salva con unos duros. No me importa ponerle los cuernos.
> Lo que me importa es sacarlo adelante. Si usted me lo cura, yo
> me lío con usted hasta que usted se harte (V, 280).

Unfortunately, Victorita's sacrifice will not be limited to that of
selling her body and experiencing the concomitant emotional stress.

Her final appearance suggests that her devotion to Paco will be cruelly rewarded with the tuberculosis that has afflicted him:

> La muchacha, por las mañanas tiene una tosecilla ligera, casi imperceptible. A veces coge algo de frío y entonces la tos se le hace un poco más ronca, como más seca (VI, 339).

Finally, two characters faced with the problem of maintaining an already precarious existence but who are seen to approach the task in contrasting fashion, are the jaded prostitute Elvira and the six-year-old gypsy singer. Apart from the obvious differences of age, sex and profession, Elvira and the *gitanito* illustrate fundamentally divergent approaches to a common problem. The child, whose age and musical efforts stir the conscience of Roberto González (II, 112), has rapidly adjusted to the rigours of the adult world in which he must fend for himself. The cost of this is manifest:

> El niño no tiene cara de persona, tiene cara de animal doméstico, de sucia bestia, de pervertida bestia de corral. Son muy pocos sus años para que el dolor haya marcado aún el navajazo del cinismo —o de la resignación— en su cara, y su cara tiene una bella e ingenua expresión estúpida, una expresión de no entender nada de lo que pasa (II, 120-1).

He accepts, as merely one of life's minor inconveniences, the fact that a drunken whore can kick him aside like a dog (II, 120). The important thing for him is that he continue his singing and his daily routine; selling his *calderilla* to bars in need of small change, eating a simple meal in a *taberna*, singing a little more, and then, in the small hours, riding "home" on the bumper of the last tram:

> El niño que canta flamenco duerme debajo de un puente, en el camino del cementerio . . . .
> El niño que canta flamenco se moja cuando llueve, se hiela si hace frío, se achicharra en el mes de agosto, mal guarecido a la escasa sombra del puente: es la vieja ley del Dios del Sinaí (VI, 341).

Elvira, having lost the charms so advantageous to the successful pursuit of her profession, is at the opposite end of working life to the *gitanito*. She appears to idle away most of her time in doña Rosa's café, chatting with doña Rosa or glancing at don Pablo, her former lover. Elvira leads "una vida perra, una vida que, bien mirado, ni merecería la pena vivirla" (I, 55); she eats poorly but tries to persuade doña Rosa otherwise, sleeps badly and, in the mornings, is reluctant to get up and face the new day. She apparently recognizes that she

can no longer afford to be selective about her clients (II, 133), and
also gives the distinct impression of being physically and mentally
drained. She undoubtedly has a lingering fondness for don Pablo and
this, combined with her general apathy, results in her cool response
to the advances of Leoncio Maestre (I, 81-3). It seems quite possible
that Elvira's future sexual experiences will be confined to the sort of
erotic nightmare that she has (IV, 245-7) and which, temporarily at
least, rekindles her waning sexual feelings. Elvira is, in effect, in the
process of giving up her struggle; she has all but succumbed to the
ravages of time and possesses neither sufficient motivation nor the
will to adjust to her changing circumstances.   Instead, she will
passively observe her own inexorable decline:

> Ahora se conforma con no ir al hospital, con poder seguir en su
> miserable fonducha; a lo mejor, dentro de unos años, su sueño
> dorado es una cama en el hospital, al lado del radiador de la
> calefacción (II, 133).

The great majority of the characters found in *La colmena* are
stereotypes receiving a varying degree of attention, who show little
development. Not even those who appear with relative frequency,
such as doña Rosa, are accorded a portrayal that suggests that Cela
has been principally concerned to probe and display personalities
being gradually developed and modified by circumstances. The brief
time span of the action, the lack of chronological sequence and the
sheer number of characters involved would impede any such intention.
Instead, narrative incident is used to illustrate certain facets of
basically static characters.   Some of these characters appear with
much more frequency than others and in the process often reveal an
attitude or quality seen for the first time or perhaps suggested in one
of the author's many biographical sketches. At times, a particular
revelation may be something of a surprise, although this is usually
not the case. In any event, it would be erroneous to suggest that Cela
accords worthlessly superficial portrayals to most of the characters in
the novel. One of his major skills is an ability to convey, implicitly
or explicitly, often by means of a small but significant statement or
action, a frame of mind or a characteristic. Thus, although the
characters of *La colmena* undeniably serve mainly to illustrate the
themes of the novel, at the same time they are normally of sufficient
interest in themselves to warrant the reader's attention.   Cela's

characterization might best be described as economical yet incisive and it certainly indicates the author's consummate ability to generate the maximum amount of interest from a limited source.

Whereas Cela's talent as a novelist has been questioned by some critics (particularly Alborg), his skill as a writer has been widely acclaimed. Thus Arturo Torres-Ríoseco writes:

> El estilo de *La colmena* es rico, variado, lleno de sabor popular y de expresiones vernáculas; usa una lengua profana, cruda, vulgar, pero de gran encanto masculino . . . Yo creo que desde los tiempos de Cervantes ningún escritor sobrepasa a Cela en la maestría del lenguaje vernacular, en la capacidad torrencial de lo lingüísticamente grotesco, en el uso del giro picaresco, del adjetivo picante y sabroso, o en el humorismo con que salpimenta sus descripciones barrocas (*16*, 68).

Nora is more concise, describing Cela as "ante todo y sin discusión posible, un gran prosista" (*8*, 68), whilst Alborg, who seriously questions the right of Cela to be regarded as the *doyen* of post-Civil War novelists, has no hesitation in praising his accomplishments as a writer:

> Cela es un escritor extraordinario por los cuatro costados: por la riqueza de su léxico, por la propiedad y precisión de sus adjetivaciones, por la fuerza y expresividad de su lenguaje, por el dominio del instrumento que maneja, por su intención y su mordacidad, por su agudeza y por su sal (*6*, 116).

Before we embark on a discussion of the main stylistic features of *La colmena*, a further comment from Cela on his novel should be mentioned. In the *Nota a la primera edición* he expresses his disdain for the attempts of those who seek a convenient pigeon-hole for each novel that falls into their hands:

> La novela no sé si es realista, o idealista, o naturalista, o costumbrista, o lo que sea. Tampoco me preocupa demasiado. Que cada cual le ponga la etiqueta que quiera: uno ya está hecho a todo (958).

With this encouragement from the author, I propose to excuse myself from any discussion of whether *La colmena* is an example of realism or naturalism, etc. Instead, having already discussed the structure of the novel and the themes and the way that the structure tends to emphasize the principal theme, that of the repetitious and monotonous nature of the lives of the characters, I now hope to indicate the salient features, as they appear in *La colmena*, of Cela the writer. The first aspect that should be discussed concerns Cela the author, that is, the relationship imposed by the author between himself and his narrative and the extent to which Cela either detaches himself from or involves himself in the narration.

The Position of the Author

D. W. Foster has discussed various aspects of the author-narrative relationship of *La colmena* and particularly the editorial notes and what he describes as "the intrusions of Cela as the author", saying that "elsewhere the author as Camilo José Cela has consistently attempted to remain outside the world of the narrative" (*9*, 72). Foster concludes: "Although Cela does not make a moral judgment on what he presents, his own position with reference to the work permits him the neutral commentary that gives the novel its depth of perception" (*9*, 76). I should like to take issue with these last two statements and suggest that, in fact, whereas Cela does on some occasions intervene directly in the narrative, he also frequently insinuates his presence to the reader. Also, whilst agreeing with Foster's choice of the word "commentary", I question his qualifying adjective and believe that Cela does feel, and often expresses, compassion for many of his characters. By the same token, he is also capable of directing both sarcasm and implied condemnation toward others.

On various occasions, the reader of *La colmena* is reminded of the presence of Cela when he quietly makes a comment in the first person, singular or plural. Thus, in the opening pages we find: "Yo creo que" (I, 49), "A mí no me parece que" (I, 50) and, referring to one of the characters, "Digo todo esto porque, a lo mejor, después vuelve a salir" (I, 68). These direct, although fairly unobtrusive, intrusions become less frequent as the narrative progresses but still serve to give the reader the occasional reminder that the author is present both as narrator and spectator:

> Un hombre baja por Goya leyendo el periódico; cuando lo cogemos pasa por delante de una pequeña librería de lance . . . (II, 114),

and "Ya dijimos en otro lado lo siguiente' (V, 315).

Apart from the many biographical sketches contained in the

novel, Cela also takes it upon himself to give additional information concerning, for example, a particular character's nature or circumstances. In this way, the author may both assert his omniscience and at the same time indicate that he is not as detached as the narrative technique that he employs might suggest. Thus, don Pablo's superficial charm belies his true nature and the author does not hesitate to inform the reader of this:

> A don Pablo le sube a la cara una sonrisa de beatitud. Si se le pudiese abrir el pecho, se le encontraría un corazón negro y pegajoso como la pez (I, 79).

Conversely, Cela exhibits a certain compassion for the circumstances of the prostitute Elvira: "La pobre no come lo bastante para ser ni viciosa ni virtuosa" (I, 98), and, more generally:

> Y algunas docenas de muchachas esperan —¿qué esperan, Dios mío?, ¿por qué las tienes tan engañadas?— con la mente llena de dorados sueños . . . (IV, 273).

It would seem that Cela cannot resist a certain involvement with many of his characters nor can he resist frequently nudging his readers in order to remind them of his presence. In this informal and informative way Cela establishes and maintains a certain casual intimacy between the reader, himself and his characters.

Repetition

One of the most consistently striking stylistic features of *La colmena* is Cela's use of repetition —ranging from the repetition of a descriptive passage or part of a dialogue (usually with slight modifications), to that of the name of the character dominating a particular narrative unit, or of a verb which serves to give a certain unity of action between consecutive units. Two examples of the first category occur with the waiter Pepe's false account to doña Rosa of his treatment of Martín Marco (I, 80 and II, 110) and the description of don Obdulio's portrait in doña Celia's *casa de citas* (III, 203 and V, 315). In both cases, the minor modifications to the repeated version are obviously deliberate and suggest that Cela is consciously trying to achieve an effect that will make the reader think carefully about perception, memory and perspective.

Cela's repetition of the names of characters within the narrative units, usually introducing each paragraph, is a feature that occurs throughout the novel. Often, each mention of the character's name will herald information concerning disposition as well as physical features, physical state or posture:

> Doña Rosa no era, ciertamente, lo que se suele decir una sensitiva . . .

> Doña Rosa sudaba por el bigote y por la frente . . .

> Doña Rosa clava sus ojitos de ratón sobre Pepe . . .

> Doña Rosa se palpa el vientre . . .

> Doña Rosa levantó la cabeza y respiró con profundidad (I, 59-60).

Other examples of this type of repetition describe, for instance, the daily routine of doña Rosa (VI, 339-40); doña Visitación's curiosity and actions when the postman brings a registered letter addressed to her daughter (V, 283); el señor Ramón's physical appearance and Spartan ways (VI, 338-9); Roberto González's thrift and stoicism (VI, 340-1), or the harsh existence and physical discomfort suffered by the *gitanito* who sings for his survival (VI, 341). This type of repetition is particularly in evidence in Chapter VI and it is no coincidence that the chapter concludes with a paragraph beginning: "La mañana, esa mañana eternamente repetida" (VI, 343). Thus, Cela's style here, like his use of structure elsewhere, serves to emphasize a theme.

Cela's repetition of a verb to give an association of action between consecutive narrative units occurs on numerous occasions. For example:

Tomar   Celestino Ortiz se levantó de su jergón, encendió la luz del bar, tomó un traguito de sifón y se metió en el retrete.
                Laurita ya se tomó su pippermint. Pablo ya se tomó un whisky (IV, 257).

Oler   La señora Paulina, golpeándose los recios muslos con las palmas de las manos, aún se acuerda de lo mal que olía el señor gordo.
                Estaba enfermo y sin un real, pero se suicidó porque olía a cebolla (V, 303).

Llamar   —Sí, descuida, yo te llamaré a ese teléfono.
                Doña Matilde llama a voces a sus huéspedes (V, 320).

In addition, there are also examples of association between narrative units that indicate a state rather than an action, using, for instance, a noun and its corresponding adjective:

> Yo sería ya una viejecita, hija mía, pero no me cabría el corazón

en el pecho, de orgullo.
    —A mí tampoco, mamá.

Martín se repone pronto, va orgulloso de sí mismo (V, 324).
A numerical association occurs with "cuatro estaciones" and "cuatro
castañas" (II, 121) and examples of the various types of repetition
mentioned here abound in *La colmena*, some less obvious than others.
Alonso Zamora Vicente states: "El sistema de repeticiones es el más
socorrido y patente de la obra de Camilo José Cela" (*15*, 191), and
on the basis of the evidence presented in *La colmena* it would indeed
be difficult to contest this judgment.

Graphic Language

One of the outstanding features of *La colmena* is the manner in
which Cela conveys, in both dialogue and description, a vivid and
often starkly realistic visual impression of characters, postures,
incidents and attitudes. Thus, almost immediately after doña Rosa's
introduction, a description of one of her favourite distractions emphasizes her general repulsiveness:

    Cuando está pensativa, se distrae y se saca virutas de la cara, largas
    a veces como tiras de serpentinas (I, 50).

Or the coarseness of Elvira is vividly suggested:

    La señorita Elvirita escupe debajo de la mesa y se seca la boca
    con la vuelta de un guante (I, 62),

whilst the physical appearance of the *gitanito* is described in such a
way as to clearly indicate that his existence has already forged an
animal rather than a human being:

    El niño no tiene cara de persona, tiene cara de animal doméstico,
    de sucia bestia, de pervertida bestia de corral (II, 120).

In less vigorous yet equally effective language doña Asunción is
described as having "un condescendiente aire de oveja" (I, 86).
Popular phrases not intended to describe character or attitudes but
used rather for graphic effect include examples dealing with the
weather: "—Estoy helado. Hace un frío como para destetar hijos de
puta" (II, 128); a fatal illness: "—El tiene un cáncer como una casa"
(III, 205); or, perhaps, a café musician taking some bicarbonate of
soda: "Los mastica como si fueran nueces y después bebe un sorbito
de agua" (I, 94).

The uninhibited and callous frankness of a child is exhibited in a
passage in which the visual effect suggests a rather sinister humour:

> —No, a ese señor no le huele la boca a goma podrida. Le huele
> a lombarda y a pies. Si yo fuese de ese señor me pondría una vela
> derretida en la nariz. Entonces hablaría como la prima Emilita
> —gua, gua—, que la tienen que operar de la garganta. Mamá dice
> que cuando la operen de la garganta se le quitará esa cara de boba
> que tiene y ya no dormirá con la boca abierta. A lo mejor, cuando
> la operen se muere. Entonces la meterán en una caja blanca,
> porque aún no tiene tetas ni lleva tacón (I, 95-6).

With reference to the struggle for survival or that against tedium, the
new morning or new day are dramatically visualized as either parasitic or predatory:

> La mañana sube, poco a poco, trepando como un gusano por
> los corazones de los hombres y de las mujeres de la ciudad (VI,
> 342).

> Miles de hombres se duermen abrazados a sus mujeres sin
> pensar en el duro, en el cruel día que quizás les espere, agazapado
> como un gato montés, dentro de tan pocas horas (IV, 273).

This type of simile is also employed to describe the wind at night,
while the night itself appears to help foster the hunger that the day
has witnessed:

> La calle, al cerrar de la noche, va tomando un aire entre
> hambriento y misterioso, mientras un vientecillo que corre como
> un lobo, silba por entre las casas (IV, 223).

Cela rarely indulges in descriptions of the city itself and whilst the
streets of Madrid are referred to by name on countless occasions and
whilst there are also frequent mentions of particular Metro stations,
buildings and monuments, the lack of description of the urban
environment makes it impossible for someone unacquainted with
Madrid to visualize the city. The author is primarily interested in
describing characters, attitudes, incidents and atmospheres and leaves
the physical background almost entirely to the imagination of the
reader.

Humour

Although *La colmena* presents a largely bleak and pessimistic
picture of the problems and attitudes of a section of 1943 Madrid
society, the novel does contain frequent moments of humour.
Examples are numerous and varied. Characters may be the object of
Cela's sarcasm:

> . . . la señorita Elvira deja caer la colilla y la pisa. La señorita

Elvira, de cuando en cuando, tiene gestos de verdadera princesa (I, 64).

or may have a particular failing ridiculed. Thus, the progress of don Ibrahím's pompous rhetoric is interrupted by two comments from the flat next door, both on the mundane subject of a child's bowel movements:

—¿Ha hecho su caquita la nena? (II, 145).

El vecino de al lado preguntaba por el color. Su mujer le decía que de color normal (II, 150).

There are also instances when a character is seen indulging in some small, intimate pleasure which may have, for example, humorous associations: "Lola se rasca el ombligo y después se huele el dedo" (V, 314).

At times, the humour is fairly crude, as when, for instance, a young child recounts a comical incident concerning a pair of soiled underpants (I, 95), and sometimes it centres around a comic incident which may possess certain macabre qualities. When, for example, doña Juana indicates that her deceased husband was a righteous man, Cela immediately informs to the contrary:

El difunto marido de doña Juana, don Gonzalo Sisemón, había acabado sus días en un prostíbulo de tercera clase, una tarde que le falló el corazón. Sus amigos lo tuvieron que traer en un taxi, por la noche, para evitar complicaciones. A doña Juana le dijeron que se había muerto en la cola de Jesús de Medinaceli, y doña Juana se lo creyó. El cadáver de don Gonzalo venía sin tirantes, pero doña Juana no cayó en el detalle (V, 287).

Finally, mention should be made of the use of ironic humour which occurs on many occasions throughout the novel and is particularly evident in the *Final*. Here, Martín Marco's blissful ignorance of the notice of the warrant for his detention, published in the newspaper he carries, is exploited as Cela has him utter such phrases as:

—A veces, en la prensa, vienen indicaciones muy buenas para los que buscamos empleo (*Final*, 357), and

—Hoy verán los míos que soy otro hombre . . .

Se palpa el periódico y sonríe.

— ¡Aquí puede haber una pista! (*Final*, 359).

This brief outline of the main stylistic features of *La colmena* can be no more than an indication of Cela's skill as a writer. An appreciation of the carefully wrought structure of the novel and the way in which theme and structure complement each other should not distract the reader from the quality of Cela's writing, whether it be for description or for dialogue. With regard to the latter, it is important to realize that the intimacy that Cela exhibits with his characters, their idiosyncrasies and attitudes, also embraces their language. Far more evident than even the formal stylistic features of *La colmena* is the popular language of Madrid that permeates the entire novel. This language includes extensive use of diminutives, popular expressions, slang and obscenities. It is a vital and often comical or crude language. But most important of all, it is the primary means by which these people express their fears and hostilities or try to dissimulate their anxiety and insecurity. As such it is obviously an important part of the life of Madrid at the time and an inescapable feature of *La colmena* —a feature which should be appreciated as a richly varied, basic ingredient of the novel, rather than be subjected to a lexical autopsy.

VIII   Conclusion

La colmena is a challenging work which requires a good deal of diligence and patience on the part of the reader. The difficulties presented by the novel are most readily overcome when the reader is prepared to accept the fact that a developing plot, character development and what might be termed narrative progress are not, nor are intended to be, fundamental features of the work. Cela has said enough in his *Notas* to the various editions of *La colmena* and also in other essays to suggest that the author himself is fully aware that this novel —if, indeed, one may be permitted to apply the term "novel"— does not fit comfortably and easily into any of the many compartments that constitute the genre. In fact, Cela often gives the impression of being excessively preoccupied —even to the point of defensiveness or sensitivity— with defining or justifying this particular work. Cavalier he may frequently be, yet beneath the veneer of confidence or even arrogance it is not difficult to detect a measure of insecurity in the author. Cela has indicated the amount of time and effort dedicated to *La colmena* and is, perhaps, occasionally apprehensive that both the purpose of his novel and the technical feat involved might not receive the favourable attention that they merit. Yet, although Cela has his detractors, at the same time a large majority of critics recognize and proclaim the qualities and value of *La colmena*.

The main technical achievement of the novel lies in the skilful synthesis of structure, theme and style. In addition, and without resorting to the creation of a plot or dramatic movement, and also without the assistance of carefully developed characters, Cela has succeeded in illustrating the problems, frustrations and diversions of a section of 1943 Madrid society. The structure, style and tone of *La colmena* constantly remind the reader of the largely monotonous existences of the people presented in the narrative. Even the more fortunate of this society are shown to be engaged in a rather pathetic and ultimately futile struggle with the corrosive and apparently invincible forces that assail them. There are, of course, glimmers of hope —the attitude of Roberto and Filo González or el señor Ramón and a few others might inspire some optimism. But the qualities that such characters exhibit are, in reality, little more than the "grito en el desierto" which Cela terms his novel in the *Nota a la segunda edición* (959).

If *La colmena* has a weakness, it might be that the structure tends to distract the unwary reader from the thematic content and intention of the work. Yet this apparent weakness is, in fact, one of the main strengths of *La colmena* and the most obvious reiteration of the principal theme —that of the monotonous and repetitious nature of the lives of those encountered in post-Civil War Madrid.

Although Cela has written much since 1951, including several novels, he has yet to match the achievement of *La colmena*. Both *Mrs. Caldwell habla con su hijo* (1953) and *La catira* (1955) received a good deal of attention but generated a largely unenthusiastic or even hostile response from critics. In the late 1950s and during the 1960s, Cela devoted a considerable amount of his time and efforts to *Papeles de Son Armadans*, short stories, other collections, and literary criticism. By the mid 1960s many were beginning to wonder not what had become of Cela, for his new work was readily published although the merit of much of it was questioned, but rather where was the manifestation of the talent that had produced *La familia de Pascual Duarte*, *Viaje a la Alcarria* or *La colmena*. José Marra-López expressed a fairly widespread concern and curiosity when, in 1964, he wrote:

> Lo que sí es evidente es que, desde *La colmena*, Camilo José Cela no ha escrito otra obra de tal importancia dentro de su producción. Pero no ocurre sólo eso, sino también que la crítica, durante estos últimos años, además de lamentarse por sus inhibiciones, predecía justamente graves peligros a la obra celiana a la vista de los varios libros que publica cada año y la naturaleza de éstos. Ha llegado un momento que parece crítico para el escritor, para su futuro como tal, dado que, incluso su incomparable prosa, parece haber encallado en una problemática encrucijada.[8]

In the late 1960s the knowledge that Cela was writing a major novel connected with the Spanish Civil War provoked a cautious optimism and when *San Camilo, 1936* appeared in 1969, the reviewer for the

---

[8] "El 'celismo' de Camilo José Cela", *Insula*, Núm. 215 (Oct. 1964), p. 13.

Times Literary Supplement commented:

> For too many years C. J. Cela has been squandering his skills on collections of a distinctive but meatless journalism and novels perversely restricted to a pathology of human decay and loneliness . . . the publication of *San Camilo, 1936* is an encouraging event. It represents a definite recovery of nerve in Spain's most gifted living novelist.[9]

Unfortunately, Cela's rather restricted account of life in Madrid during the first week or so of the Civil War, whilst perhaps suggesting that the novelist had regained his nerve, did not suggest that he had regained the mastery that he exhibits in *La colmena*. *San Camilo, 1936* is a powerful but gruelling novel that lacks the artistic subtleties of *La colmena*, yet even so it should be ranked as one of Cela's more important achievements.

It is to be hoped that there is still much more to come from Cela and that his skills may be particularly directed toward the task of writing novels. He will, however, find it difficult to match the quality and agility that he attains in *La colmena* and which make it, to date, the finest novel to have emerged from post-Civil War Spain.

[9] "A Mirror in Madrid", *TLS*, 2 April 1970, p. 355.

Bibliographical Note

Social and Historical Background

1. Crozier, Brian. *Franco: A Biographical History*. London, 1967. A dispassionate view of Franco which includes a brief but starkly impressive account of the terror of the post-Civil War years.
2. Hamilton, Thomas. *Appeasement's Child: The Franco Regime in Spain*. New York, 1943. An interesting eye-witness account of life in Spain during the years immediately following the end of the Civil War. Overtly anti-Franco, with a great deal of proselytizing.
3. Hills, George. *Spain*. London, 1970. Contains a useful description of social, economic and political problems in post-Civil War Spain.
4. Payne, Stanley. *Franco's Spain*. New York, 1967. Particularly strong on economic problems and development, and social change since 1939.
5. Thomas, Hugh. *The Spanish Civil War*. Harmondsworth, 1965. An excellent account of the causes and course of the war. Suffers at times from overly detailed descriptions of minor actions and exploits. Also contains a brief but good account of the aftermath of the war.

General Studies

6. Alborg, Juan Luis. *Hora actual de la novela española*. Madrid, 1958. Attacks Cela's talent as a novelist with a gusto that suggests personal animosity. He does, however, proclaim Cela's skill as a writer. Should be balanced against Zamora Vicente's eulogy of the novels of Cela.
7. Brown, Gerald. *A Literary History of Spain: The Twentieth Century*, London, 1972. A fine account of literary currents and trends in twentieth-century Spain. Cela and the post-Civil War novel could have been accorded a little more attention.
8. Nora, Eugenio de. *La novela española contemporánea. III*. Madrid, 1970. In a few pages, Nora skilfully indicates the principal structural and thematic features of *La colmena*. The section on Cela is an excellent introduction to the novelist's work.

Critical Studies

9. Foster, David W. *Forms of the Novel in the Work of Camilo José Cela*. Columbia, Missouri, 1967. The chapter on *La colmena* provides a good analysis of the structure of the novel. There are occasional inaccuracies and contradictions but these do not seriously detract from the overall merit of Foster's description of the formal aspects of the novel.
10. Ilie, Paul. *La novelistica de Camilo José Cela*. Madrid, 1963. The chapter on *La colmena* is good. At times, however, Ilie does indulge in some questionable generalizations or fails to develop many of his thoughtful observations.
11. Kirsner, Robert. *The Novels and Travels of Camilo José Cela*. Chapel Hill, North Carolina, 1966. A rather windy and superficial piece of criticism. Kirsner makes some good points concerning *La colmena* but his frequent inaccuracies in both general and specific comments indicate

a lack of real familiarity with the novel.

12.   McPheeters, D. W. *Camilo José Cela*. New York, 1969. Contains an excellent chapter on *La colmena* which is probably the most useful introduction to this novel yet written.

13.   Ortega, José. "El sentido temporal en *La colmena*", *Symposium*, XIX, No. 2 (Summer 1965), 115-22. A useful study of some of the more obvious temporal aspects of the novel.

14.   Spires, Robert C. "Cela's *La colmena*: The Creative Process as Message", *Hispania* (U.S.A.), LV, No. 4 (December 1972), 873-80. A perceptive study, mainly restricted to the first chapter of the novel, of temporal and tonal aspects of *La colmena*.

15.   Zamora Vicente, Alonso. *Camilo José Cela: Acercamiento a un escritor.* Madrid, 1962. Zamora Vicente makes the obvious points in this general study. The chapters on *La colmena* and on Cela's style are useful introductions to the novel and the author.

16.   Hispanic Institute in the United States. *Camilo José Cela: Vida y obra—Bibliografía—Antología*. New York, 1962. Contains several general articles, the best of which is that by Castellet, as well as an interesting "Relativo Curriculum Vitae" by Cela himself, a bibliography to 1962 and also an anthology of Cela's prose and poetry.